The
Tiger
of
Bitter Valley

By Norma R. Youngberg

Illustrated by Harold Munson

TEACH Services, Inc.
P U B L I S H I N G
www.TEACHServices.com

Copyright © 2013 Norma Youngberg and TEACH Services, Inc.
ISBN-13: 978-1-47960-028-1 (Paperback)
ISBN-13: 978-1-47960-029-8 (ePub)
ISBN-13: 978-1-47960-030-4 (Kindle/Mobi)

Library of Congress Control Number: 2012949795

Published by

TEACH Services, Inc.
P U B L I S H I N G
www.TEACHServices.com

Table of Contents

For
Rhoda and Elmo
and
their children

1.
The Magic Mark

THE BOY DREW HIS GREEN AND YELLOW SARONG close about his body and slipped into the brush beside the path. Those voices he heard, just round the curve of the path, sounded strange. He hid in the bushes and peered out, watching, until two men came into sight. One was young and tall; the other was an older man, short and fat. The boy remembered having seen the fat one at the market place beside the lake.

The fear he had felt on first hearing the strange voices passed away when he saw that they were men of his own tribe. Now he was curious about them. Why had they come?

Stepping out into the path, he greeted them according to the polite custom of his people: "Peace to your coming."

"Peaceful morning," they answered.

"You are the chief's son?" the older man asked, eying the boy's rajah scarf. "I am the chief's son," the boy replied. "Will you take us to your father? We have important business with him." The men looked so solemn that the boy felt his fear returning. What could these men want with his father?

He led the visitors along the path till they came to the old houses built on platforms above the ground, with steep-pitched, sway-backed roofs. Rocky Hills Village was large and old. The boy's grandfather had been chief there for many years. When he died, the boy's father had become chief. The people were peaceful and contented. The boy wondered if these men brought trouble. Had they come about the road tax? Evidently some serious matter was troubling them—something important.

"Perhaps you would like to see Gadoh, our witch doctor, too," he suggested. Everyone in the village feared and respected Gadoh and his charms. If this business was serious, he should know about it.

"Yes, I suppose he might as well come along with us." The older man spoke with some impatience. "Call him. This concerns the whole village."

They stopped at Gadoh's door, and the boy shouted his name. The witch man came out with a suspicious look in his eyes. He stared at the two strangers with cool indifference. "What do you want of me?" he inquired.

"We have an important business to bring before Chief Feermin. It is an urgent matter, which concerns the whole village. Since you are the medicine man, perhaps you had better come with us."

Gadoh was a young-looking man with a fine, smooth skin and a bushy head of coarse hair. He was stocky and strong. The expression on his face was one of studied insolence. Now he deliberately squatted in the door of his house and took out his *ciri* box. He rolled himself a quid of betel nut and stuffed it into his mouth. He settled the black velvet cap on his unruly hair and rearranged his handsome shoulder scarf. Then, still eying the two men with distaste, he stood up, stretched his thick legs, and followed them to the chief's house.

In spite of the peaceful greetings that were exchanged, the boy knew that his father was surprised and puzzled by this unexpected visit. The two visitors were given clean mats to sit on, and the betel nut was passed around. The men acted friendly.

"You have a fine, strong son here." The older man patted the boy's shoulder. "What is his name?"

"He has no name yet," the chief answered. "He is already thirteen years old, but we still call him Doyli-Doyli." The men laughed, because Doyli-Doyli is a common name for all young boys and means Sonny Boy.

The chief spoke again. "I will not give him a name until I can find one that means something great. One day something will happen to show me what his name must be."

For a few minutes nothing more was said. The little group all helped themselves to more betel nut and chewed together peacefully for a while before inquiring about the business the visitors had brought.

The boy looked at his father. The chief's dark face was stern. His big hands fumbled with the betel nut while his keen eyes searched the faces of the two men. He sat cross-legged on the rajah mat, his beautiful hand-woven rajah scarf folded over his right shoulder. His pleated turban rested at a striking angle on his thick black hair. He was a true Mamora—a prince of the Battak tribe of northern Sumatra.

"Chief Feermin"—the older man broke the silence—"we have brought you something powerful and very important. It is for your whole village. It will be a blessing and a protection, but it will cause you and all your people some pain and inconvenience."

The chief leaned forward on his mat, his dark eyes afire. The boy could see relief on his face. "Show it to me! If it is for the good of our village, I will accept it."

Gadoh, the medicine man, spat a mouthful of betel-nut juice on the floor and frowned.

"It is a new medicine," the younger man explained. "It has come to us from Europe—a country across the ocean. It is a medicine against the terrible *chachar* sickness (smallpox)."

At the mention of a new medicine, the witch doctor's eyes gleamed with anger. "We don't want any medicine from Europe in this village!" he said.

The older of the two visitors turned toward the chief, disregarding Gadoh's words. "It has been used in many cities and villages in other countries, as well as here. In the places where every person uses this medicine, the *chachar* sickness does not come."

"Does one eat this medicine?" the chief asked.

"No, no. We have a small knife. We scratch a place on the skin of the arm and spread the medicine on the scratched place."

Gadoh snorted. "What nonsense! How can scratching people's arms and spreading medicine on them keep away the *chachar?*" He glared at Chief Feermin. "I'm astonished that you even listen to such stupid foolishness!"

The older visitor looked troubled, but he continued to speak in a patient voice. "This year there is a great deal of the sickness in these mountains. In some villages every person has died. The government is urging all the chiefs to allow their people to have the medicine."

"Don't bring it here!" Gadoh screamed, springing to his feet. He shook his fist at the two men. "This is foreign magic. It is the work of devils! It will cause madness! It will kill all our children! I know about that medicine!" The witch doctor turned his back and stalked away in hot anger. He scrambled down the ladder to the ground, and strode off.

The two visitors looked at Chief Feermin with worried eyes. "It is the medicine men who cause delay and make trouble about this medicine. It is the same in every village. The lives of all your people are at stake. Have any of our witch men ever been able to prevent or cure this *chachar* sickness?"

"I suppose you have brought some of this medicine with you," the chief said, after a thoughtful pause.

"We have some," they answered. The younger man showed them a long, slender bottle filled with a cloudy-looking liquid, like the juice from a young coconut.

"Then you may make the medicine on my body first," Chief Feermin told them. "I am rajah of this village. It is a large one. It is right that I should try the medicine first and see what it will do to me."

The older man took the bottle in his hand. "After we scratch your arm and put the medicine on it, you will feel nothing for three or four days. Then the arm may swell and ache. The place where the knife has scratched will become a sore, something like a boil. Your whole body may be sick and feverish. Do not be afraid. This will pass away in a few days. The swelling will go down. The arm will get well, and the scab from the sore will fall off. It will leave a deep mark. This is the magic sign that protects all who have it from the *chachar* sickness."

Both of the visitors held out their arms, where deep scars showed on the skin, and the younger man spoke. "Now we can walk in the villages where the sickness is raging. We can take care of the dying and bury the dead. We have no fear of the *chachar*."

Chief Feermin held out his arm. With a tiny knife, the older man scratched the skin until the blood began to ooze out. Then he smeared a little of the medicine on the scratched spot. "Blow your breath on it till it is dry," he said. "Be sure not to cover your arm with anything, and don't touch it or scratch it."

"Now you will make the medicine for my son," the chief said.

Doyli-Doyli heard these words with terror. He remembered all that Gadoh had said about this new medicine from across the sea. He wanted to run away and hide, but he knew that no Mamora runs from danger. He was the only son of Chief Feermin—a prince of the Battak tribe. He held out his arm for the scratching.

"If this medicine is good for me and my son, if everything happens as you have said, then all my village will receive the medicine." The chief looked sternly at the two men as they put their knife and bottle of medicine away in a little bag. "I will call you when the time comes." Chief Feermin rose from his mat.

The visitors rose also. "You will find us in the village by the lake. Do not delay." The older man looked grave. "Any day the *chachar* may come to Rocky Hills Village. Then many will die, and most of those who live will be terribly disfigured."

The Tiger of Bitter Valley

"I will call you at the right time," the chief said, dismissing the visitors.

In a few days Doyli-Doyli's arm became sore and swollen. His body was hot with fever, and he ached all over. The chief felt sick also, and for two days he lay on his mat, while his wife begged him to send for the witch doctor.

"No, no," he insisted. "This will pass away. It is just as I expected it would be. Don't worry about Doyli-Doyli. He will be all right in a few days."

So no one told Gadoh that the chief and his son had received the foreign medicine. If he noticed the sores on their arms he said nothing. Sores and boils were a common sight in the village.

In a few days the fever and sickness went away, and the swelling disappeared. After several more days the sore dried up, and at last even the scab fell off; and Doyli-Doyli thought no more about the foreign medicine.

It was at this time that the chief decided to make a trip. "I will go to look for water buffaloes," he told his family. "I want to buy two good strong ones before it is time for us to plow our rice fields." Then he set out.

The boy missed his father greatly. Usually he was allowed to go with him. Now he spent most of his time in the kitchen room of the house with his mother and his two little sisters. The chief was away for four days. When he returned he was leading two fine young buffaloes.

Chief Feermin did not say where he had been, but he looked sad and troubled. The next morning he visited every house in the village, looking at the children and talking to the people. The worried look never left his face. Doyli-Doyli knew there must be something his father feared.

The following day the big three-day market at the village on the lake shore began. Gadoh came back from the market in a fierce rage. He called loudly in front of Chief Feermin's door. "Does the chief of Rocky Hills Village intend to spread the *chachar* sickness among us?" he asked in a voice of controlled fury.

10

"No. On the contrary, I intend to protect all our people from the *chachar* sickness." Chief Feermin smiled at the witch man's anger.

"Then is it your intention to allow the foreign medicine to be made on the people of this village?"

"Gadoh"—the chief took him by the arm—"you have made medicine for this village for as many years as I have been chief. Your medicine is strong, and your charms are powerful; but you have never discovered how to make medicine against the terrible *chachar* sickness. No medicine man in all our villages knows how to do it. Is it not right and wise for us to accept the medicine from across the sea when we have none of our own?"

The anger of Gadoh was terrible to see. He jerked away from the chief. His face grew purple with rage. Uttering oaths and curses, he left the chief's presence, swinging his heavy arms in gestures of helpless fury.

Doyli-Doyli trembled. "Father, Father!" He took hold of his father's hand. "Gadoh is so angry! Are you not afraid?"

"No, my son." Chief Feermin looked at his son with affection. "I am not afraid." He held out his arm for the boy to look at. "Do you see that mark?" he said. "It is a magic mark." He lifted the boy's arm and examined the new scar.

"Those who have this magic mark need not fear the *chachar* sickness."

"Are you sure, Father?" Doyli-Doyli asked.

"Yes, I am sure. When I went to buy the water buffaloes I entered a village where many people have been dying of the *chachar*. It is a dreadful sight." Pain filled the chief's eyes. "I helped to bury the dead. It is a horrible thing! I never knew it would be like that." He paused, and the room was very quiet. It seemed that he spoke with a great effort. "I saw ... Oh, my son, I cannot tell you what I saw. But this I can tell you: there were men in that village who had the magic mark. They had been there for many days. They walked safely in the midst of the horror. Then I knew. I knew that only the mark stood between me and terrible death. I knew that we must bring the medicine to all the people of our village."

"Does Gadoh know you went to that village?"

"Yes. He must have found out at the market today."

"But Father," the boy said, "there are other things to fear besides the *chachar* sickness. Gadoh may become your enemy. Perhaps he—"

"Yes, I know," the chief said. "He will try to turn all our people against this new magic. We have no time to lose. I must go to the village by the lake tomorrow. I must find the two visitors and ask them to make the medicine on the arms of all our people."

"There are still two days more of the big market near the village by the lake," Doyli-Doyli said. "May I go with you?"

"You may go," his father replied. "We will hurry now and load the buffalo cart with sugar cane. We will start for the market before sunrise tomorrow morning."

2.
The Market

IT WAS AN HOUR AFTER MIDNIGHT WHEN DOYLI-Doyli felt his father's hand on his shoulder and heard his voice. "Come, my son. We must start now if we expect to reach the market by sunrise."

The boy sat up on his mat and rubbed his eyes. Soon he could see a little in the darkness, and he hunted around on the floor and found his green velvet cap and his rajah scarf. He had laid out a clean sarong, too. Now he draped it about him, pulling it tightly around his waist, as he followed his father down the ladder and out of the big house. His mother and the little girls still slept.

Out on the green runway that served as a village street the loaded cart awaited them. The water buffalo was already hitched between the shafts; and without talking, the two climbed to the crude seat in the cart. They jogged off down the path in the light of the moon, now three quarters full. When the path joined a larger road, they overtook another buffalo cart, and soon another one came up behind them. Before the first hour of their journey had passed, there was a long string of the little roofed carts rolling clumsily along on their way to the big market by the lake. They traveled at the rate of about two miles an hour.

The boy peered about in the moonlight. The familiar countryside looked strange under the night sky. He knew that a village lay in the shadow of the hill ahead of them. He knew that a tiger had been trapped in the thick jungle of this valley. His father had killed the savage creature with a short spear.

The rice fields on the terraced hillsides gave off a rich, sweet smell in the damp darkness. A dog barked in a distant coconut garden. The boy's eyes grew heavy. He leaned against his father and drifted into sleep. The chief slept too. Every driver in the long procession dozed and rested, while the man in the first cart led the way. There was no danger that any of the big, patient buffaloes would change pace or try to pass the cart ahead. The sleepy line of carts followed the winding paths around and between the hills, sometimes skirting chasms. Still the drivers slept, comfortable and secure.

"Look! There is the lake!"

Doyli-Doyli awakened with a start at the sound of his father's voice. He sat up straight. Morning had come. The sun had not yet risen in the sky, but it was just behind the purple rim of Samosir, the great island that lies in the middle of Lake Toba. They were in sight of the market place.

The chief turned his buffalo out of the line of carts and drove down to the lake shore, where soft green grass grew thick and long. There he unhitched the buffalo, tethered him to one of the heavy wheels of the cart, and left him to crop the grass. "Now we shall have to carry some of this sugar cane over to the market place," the chief said.

They both filled their arms with the fat lengths of sugar cane and carried it to a spot where many people would be passing by. "This is enough for a sample," the chief said. "Perhaps I can sell it all to one buyer. You go back and keep watch over the cane that we left in the cart. Otherwise it will certainly be stolen."

The boy ran back to the cart. He pushed the cane forward, so he could sit in the back of the cart with his legs dangling. There was more light now, and the road along the lake shore was full of carts and many people on foot, hurrying toward the market place.

15

The Tiger of Bitter Valley

A fleet of fishing boats pulled in to shore, close to the spot where Doyli-Doyli sat. He knew they had been out all night after fish-the golden carp so abundant in the lake. The fisherman unloaded their catch and spread the fish out for the customers to see. The carp were beautiful to look at and good for eating, too. The tangy smell of the lake filled the boy's nostrils. The smell came from the fish and the fishermen, and he liked it. Some of the golden carp were four or five feet long. They sparkled and glittered in the clear morning light. The sun was just showing its dazzling circle above Samosir.

The boy swung his feet and watched the brown fishermen dragging the slippery fish from the boats and laying them in neat rows on the grass. He was so absorbed in watching that the chief was back at the cart before he saw him. A Chinese merchant was with him.

"You see!" the chief said. "In all the land of Toba there is no finer cane than this. Its sweetness is beyond description!"

"It appears very poor to me." The fat *towky* picked up one of the stalks and bit into it. "This is scarcely sweet at all." He spat and frowned. "I will not give you more than three guilders for the lot."

"I wouldn't think of selling for less than six guilders!" the chief said. And he turned his back, looking as if he were very much interested in the fish displayed on the grass.

"I tell you," said the Chinese merchant, raising his voice, "your sugar cane is the poorest I have seen this year. I will not give you more than three and a half guilders for it!"

The chief walked slowly toward the fish, but flung back a few angry words over his shoulder. "In all Toba there is no cane so fine as mine. I will never part with it for less than five and a half guilders!"

Now the Chinese *towky* became furious. His face grew red, and his fat chin quivered with excitement. "For a lot of useless garbage, such as this, I can offer you no more than four guilders!"

The chief had almost reached the first row of fish. He shouted back in a thunderous voice, "Go back to your shop. I cannot do business with you! I will never sell for less than five guilders!"

"I will give you four and a half-not one cent more!" the merchant screamed.

The chief turned around and came back. Both men smiled and nodded to one another. The bargain was made. They were satisfied, and the best of friends.

The Chinese *towky* had skin of a pale-yellow color, almost white. Doyli-Doyli looked at the man's naked arm with surprise. There was a deep scar on his upper arm—the magic mark! He opened his mouth to say something about it, then decided that it would not be polite. He waited until the merchant had gone to fetch his coolie, who would help him to remove the cane. Then he exclaimed, "Father! Father! Did you see? That man has the magic mark!" The boy twisted his arm around until he could look at his own magic mark. It was not as big as the Chinese man's, but it showed up better on the brown skin.

"Most of the Chinese people have the mark," Chief Feermin explained. "They are glad to have it, because in past years thousands of them died of the *chachar*. Now the mark protects them."

In a few minutes the Chinese *towky* came back with his coolie and took the cane away to his shop. Doyli-Doyli noticed that the coolie also had the magic mark.

After the Chinese merchant had paid for the cane and the cart was empty, Chief Feermin turned to his son. "Now our business with the sugar cane is done," he said, "but the most important business is not yet begun. I must find two men— the two who brought the *chachar* medicine to our village."

He pulled some coins from the bag at his belt. "Run along and have a good look at the market place," he told Doyli-Doyli, placing the coins in his hand. "Buy yourself some cakes if you find some that look good."

The market place was a wide meadow that bordered the lake. There were no buildings there. Hundreds of people came with the fruit or vegetables or other goods they hoped to sell. They brought along mats and sheets of palm leaf to make rude shelters where they could protect their wares and sit in comfort while customers came to look at their goods.

The Tiger of Bitter Valley

The boy was delighted with the market. He tried to look in every direction at once. Huge baskets of duck eggs stood in the runways between the stalls. Live chickens and ducks were squawking and fluttering in their big, coarse baskets of woven bamboo. He saw some birds that looked like enormous ducks, but around their bills they had folds of red flesh that hung down in wattles. He knew they were very expensive. They were called *serati*.

Yards and yards of bright-colored cloth fluttered from poles or lay in folded piles on the mats of the cotton sellers. Big bunches of gladioli and carnations stood in kerosene tins full of water. The air was heavy with smells—sweet and sour, tempting and revolting.

In front of one stall the boy found two large baskets of brown beetles. He stopped, fascinated by the crawling, wriggling insects. The old woman who sold them measured out the beetles with a tin can and tied the squirming mass up so skillfully that not one beetle could escape.

"Would you like to have some?" The boy looked up in surprise and found his father beside him.

The chief nodded to the old woman and handed her a coin. "We shall have them for our supper tonight," he said, looking up at the sun, which was now past midheaven. The vendor of beetles wrapped them cleverly in a green leaf and gave the wriggling parcel to the boy, who tied it in a corner of his rajah scarf.

Then he looked up at his father. "Did you find the men yet?" he asked.

"I did not find them yet. I must go and look again. I just noticed you standing here and came over to see what you were looking at. Now you must go and buy yourself some cakes."

Doyli-Doyli found the stalls where fried-banana and sweet-potato cakes were being dipped from kettles of smoking coconut oil. After going from stall to stall, sniffing the hot-grease smell in the air, he chose one where the smell of coconut oil was pure and sweet. He didn't like cakes fried in rancid oil. He watched the woman dip bananas in a rich duck-egg batter and drop them into the hot fat.

18

"Are you hungry for some cakes?" the rosy-cheeked woman asked him.

"I would like some of the fried-banana cakes and some of the sweet-potato ones, too." He showed her his two-and-one-half cent coins.

The woman laughed and selected some choice cakes for him. Doyli-Doyli munched on these delicacies, enjoying himself. The afternoon passed quickly. It was soon evening, and the chief returned to the market place. He had located the two men he had been searching for, and they were waiting now in one of the government offices.

Chief Feermin took his son by the hand and they went to the office. The men welcomed them. After betel nut had been passed around and everyone was comfortable, the chief spoke.

"I want you to come to our village and bring enough medicine to make the magic mark on all our people," he said.

"How many are there in your village?"

"There must be over a hundred men, women, and little children altogether." The chief considered the matter thoughtfully. "Can the medicine be made for the small children?"

"Yes. Even small babies must have the medicine, for they can catch the *chachar* sickness as easily as grown people."

"Then bring enough for all," Chief Feermin said.

"And the witch doctor? Will he make trouble?" The older man looked a little worried. "I am the chief. He cannot prevent this." Chief Feermin looked stern.

"We will come in seven days from this one," the older man promised. "That will give you time to persuade your people—and the witch doctor as well."

It was now past sundown—too late to start for home. The market would last another day, and there was much the chief wanted to see, and many old friends to meet and gossip with. He decided that they would spend the night in the buffalo cart and return home the following day.

They went down to the lake shore, and the chief loosened the buffalo's tether so that he could go to the edge of the lake and wallow in the soft mud. The cart was empty, except for a grass mat rolled away under the seat.

The Tiger of Bitter Valley

They built a campfire, and the chief roasted the beetles. Once their hard wings were picked off, they had a nutty flavor. With the beetles they ate rice cakes, which the chief had purchased at the market. The boy was hungry. Everything tasted very good.

"We shall use the cart for a bed," the chief said, as he climbed in and began to unroll the grass mat. "There is room enough for both of us to lie here, side by side. The night is warm. We don't need blankets." They lay with their heads toward the closed front end of the cart and their feet toward the back, which was open.

During the night the boy awakened. The moon shone brightly, but it was not the moonlight that had awakened him. Something was moving along the lake shore. The chief was awake too. Neither father nor son made a sound, or moved so much as an eyelash. A large tiger was approaching the buffalo cart.

The great beast moved quietly on padded feet. He came directly to the cart where the chief and his son were lying, petrified with horror. He sniffed at the boy's feet. Doyli-Doyli could feel the sharp whiskers prick his bare skin. The tiger's hot breath warmed his toes. He was seized with a strong desire to jerk his feet away; but he knew that if he made the slightest movement the tiger would spring on him at once.

There was no escape! He suppressed a shudder. He held his body rigid. Now the tiger stuck out his tongue. It was harsh and moist. He licked the sole of the boy's right foot. A shriek of terror pressed up in Doyli-Doyli's throat. He could hardly restrain it. Then the tiger sniffed the chief's feet. These also failed to please him; and he moved on to the lake shore, to look for food more suited to his taste.

After the tiger had gone, they both sat up, trembling. "My son," the chief said, "there are no feet like yours in all the world!" He felt the boy's feet. One was still damp from the tiger's tongue. "You must have the magic of the tigers in your blood!" His rasping breath came fast. "For this I will make a name feast!" He covered the boy's feet with the rajah scarf he usually wore on his shoulder. "For this," he repeated, "I will make such a name feast as has never been seen in our village before!"

3.
The Name Feast

LATE THE FOLLOWING MORNING THE LITTLE
roofed cart was jogging along the mountain road toward
home. The chief had gone to the market and bought supplies
for the coming feast, and the cart was heavily loaded. There
were baskets of live chickens, and a hundred duck eggs. There
was red *pooloot* and white *pooloot* and black *pooloot*, the sticky
rice from which cakes were made. There was sugar and salt
and onions. Chief Feermin had also left an order for six of the
large golden carp from the lake. These were to be delivered to
his village on the sixth morning after this one.

"It will be a great feast!" he told the boy. "This will be the
greatest feast that has ever been held in our village. At this
time a name will be chosen for you—a wonderful name!"

Doyli-Doyli kicked his bare feet against the front of the cart
and rejoiced that he would at last have a name, like other
boys. "You told the men to bring the fish on the sixth day from
today. That is the same day the men will bring the *chachar*
medicine, isn't it?" he asked his father.

"Yes, it is, my son." Chief Feermin smiled. "I have ar-
ranged it that way, because our people will be more willing to
have their arms scratched if there is a feast in preparation."

From the moment the chief reached Rocky Hills Village, he began to make preparations for the feast. He called together the old men of the village. He called Gadoh. They all sat on mats in the big room of the chief's house—the council chamber.

"Honorable friends," the chief began, when they were all settled with quids of betel nut, "I went to the market place yesterday and spent the night there. My son was with me. During the night the king tiger came to our cart and licked my son's right foot. Then he passed on. Is this not a great sign—a very great sign? The boy must have the magic of the tigers in his blood! It is time now to make a feast for him. As you know, he is already thirteen years old and he has not yet received a name."

The men looked at one another, smiling and nodding. They looked at Doyli-Doyli, especially at his feet. Gadoh spoke. "What kind of name feast will the chief make for his son?"

"It is in my mind to make a great feast, lasting three days. I have brought some supplies from the market place. My bins are full of rice, and I have three fat buffaloes. We will butcher one on each day of the feast."

Smiles grew broader, and the men chewed hard on their quids of betel nut. A pleasant excitement filled the council chamber. Then the oldest man present lifted his voice and addressed the company. He recounted the long story of Chief Feermin's life and the good deeds he had done in Rocky Hills Village. He told of the birth of Doyli-Doyli, and finally he ended with the story of the tiger and the wonderful feet of Chief Feermin's only son. "Now"—he spread his hands in a gesture of finality—"you have heard this remarkable account. You have heard how the marvelous feet of the chief's son turned away the tiger. You have heard of the chief's good intentions to make a name feast. I counsel all of you to do all you can to prepare for this feast and make it a good one."

Then another man spoke, and another. Last of all, Gadoh spoke again. "You have all heard the good words that were spoken here. On what day will the feast begin?" He looked at Chief Feermin.

"It will begin on the sixth day from this one," the chief told them.

Doyli-Doyli was surprised that Gadoh seemed to have forgotten his anger of the day before yesterday. The boy studied the broad, dark face of the witch doctor. He saw the nervous working of Gadoh's hands and the curve of his cruel mouth, and trembled. No, he thought, Gadoh has not forgotten. He is only waiting—waiting for a chance to do some evil thing.

The next days were filled with preparations. The women of the village, led by the chief's wife, beat out quantities of the finest mountain rice. They tested the palm wine. On the day before the feast they lined joints of bamboo with tender young banana leaves. This was done by rolling the leaves, slipping them down inside the bamboo, and letting them uncurl until the leaf made a soft green lining for the tube of bamboo. Into these tubes they poured the *pooloot*, mixed with rich coconut cream. After the bamboo joints were filled with the proper amount, the mouth of each was stuffed with a soft wad of banana leaf, crumpled into a ball.

Then a roaring fire was built, and the stuffed bamboo joints were set close to the blaze. Soon they began to bubble and boil. The women watched them carefully, so that they would not cook too fast. When they were well charred they were set aside to cool. Later the women would extract the *pooloot* cakes from the joints.

Chickens were killed and curried. Some of the chicken meat was made into little spiced balls, mixed with boiled potato and duck eggs. These were fried in deep coconut oil until they were a delectable brown.

On the morning of the first feast day the men butchered the first buffalo, and the women set kettles of the meat on the fire to boil. Other kettles were filled with rice. Every person in the village gathered on the green in front of the chief's house. They were dressed in their finest sarongs and wore hand-woven beaded scarfs. The chief and his son wore their most resplendent rajah scarfs.

The meat was bubbling in the kettles, and the women tending the rice were moving it away from the fire; for it was almost ready to steam dry. All the cooking was done in the open green. The people of the village watched with keen interest.

Then a shout rang out. Everyone looked up and saw that a group of strangers had just arrived in the village. They carried six large golden carp, which they laid before the chief. The villagers gathered round to see the glistening fish, and the chief ordered the women to prepare them for the feast. "Tomorrow you will bring six more," he commanded, as he paid the men for the fish.

Doyli-Doyli recognized two of the men as the messengers who had brought the *chachar* medicine. He looked around for Gadoh. Would he recognize them? The witch doctor was bending over the largest of the fish, measuring it with his hand. The boy could not see his face.

While the people were still gathered around him, the chief stood up, raised his hand, and spoke in a loud, commanding voice. "My people, this is a great day for us. It is the first day of our name feast. It is also the day when all of us will receive the magic mark. There are two men here from the government office near the market place. They have brought medicine which they will put on your arms." He smiled at his people, and the boy's heart swelled with pride, because this kind and powerful man was his own father.

"This medicine will make a magic mark on everyone of you," the chief continued. "After you have received it, you cannot get the *chachar* sickness." He pushed back his scarf, so that everyone could see that he had the mark himself. "You may all remain right where you are now, and one by one, I will ask you to pass before these two men. After each of you receives the magic mark he may go on to the feast."

As the chief spoke, Gadoh looked up, first in surprise and then in fury. The people, commanded by their chief, were already marching up to have their arms scratched. To defy the direct command of a Mamora chief in public was contrary to the customs of the people. It could not be done—yet Gadoh did not hesitate. He stepped up to the two men, his face purple with rage. The older man was just unrolling a yellow paper. Gadoh stopped short when he saw the paper. He knew by the look of it that it was a government paper. Not only was the chief against him; the government was, too—the government of the great Belanda (Holland).

The chief's son watched with breathless excitement as the man began to speak, looking directly at Gadoh. He read from the paper: "The chief of Rocky Hills Village, Feermin Mamora, has requested that all the people in his village be vaccinated against smallpox. This is an order requesting all persons in Rocky Hills Village to follow the good words of their chief and receive the medicine which the government is furnishing you, free of cost. It is a gift from Her Majesty's government to all of you."

Gadoh's hands hung loosely at his sides. His face darkened. He shook his head several times and looked as though he was about to speak—but no words came out. Meanwhile, the people were paying no attention to him. One after another, as the chief called their names, they filed past the two men and were scratched by their tiny knives. Then they went on to the feast, blowing the medicine dry as they walked away. The witch doctor turned his back on them all and went to his house.

After everyone had received the medicine, the two men began to leave the village. As they passed Gadoh's house they called to him. "Come out, Gadoh. Everyone else has taken the medicine. Everyone in this village will have the magic mark except you. Come, now. Get your arm scratched."

Gadoh appeared at the door of his house and looked down on them, with a darkness in his face that the people had never seen there before. "I will not come!" he said. "I will not have the foreign medicine made on my body."

"All right, then," the older man said. "I will not force you. This village is far from any others and quite safe. You had better stay here, and not go to the market or anywhere else while the sickness is active. There has been a new outbreak of the

26

chachar just this week. It is likely to spread to every person who has not received the magic mark."

The witch man glared, but spoke no word; and after waiting a little, the men left the village. When they had gone, Gadoh came out of his house and mingled with the others.

The feast had begun. The rice was dished up on banana leaves. Meat was served from the big kettles. The cakes of *pooloot* looked like long green sausages. The women cut them in neat slices, and the feasters peeled the banana-leaf skin from the cakes and ate them with relish. The golden carp, which had been cooked with coconut milk and hot spices, were also ready now. They were served to everyone. It was a fine feast.

Toward evening the palm wine was served, and the rejoicing people danced and sang until late in the night. Gadoh seemed to have forgotten his anger, but Doyli-Doyli looked at him often, and twice he noticed the witch doctor's eyes on himself and his father. The gleam of hatred he saw there shocked and frightened him. He decided to tell his father about it when the feast was over.

The second day of the feast was like the first, only more joyous. Another buffalo was killed, and more golden carp were delivered. More rice was prepared, and more cakes. The people feasted and drank and sang till almost morning.

The third day was the greatest day of the feast. When afternoon came, all the village elders-both men and women-gathered at the chief's house; for this was a name feast, and a grand name was to be chosen for the chief's son. It must be a name that suited a chief and one that commemorated his experience with the tiger.

There were long and eloquent speeches. Everyone spoke of the greatness of the Mamora chiefs, and especially of the majesty of Chief Feermin and his son. The story of his experience with the tiger was told and retold in beautiful words, until it became like a poem or a song on everyone's tongue. It would be remembered for many years in the folklore of this village.

When the excitement and eloquence had reached a peak of intensity, the chief rose from his mat, and taking his son by the shoulders, he turned him so that he faced the company. Then he announced in a loud voice, "I proclaim you, my son, Menga-Rajah-Segala-Harimau—Great Ruler of all the Tigers."

"Olo!... Olo!" The musical word of consent rang out.

At last the boy had a name—a name fit for a king. Although it was a name he might find hard to live up to, it was indeed a great name. Now the speeches began all over again, but this time they were addressed to the new Ruler of all the Tigers. Only Gadoh was silent. He looked at the new Rajah of Tigers with such fixed hatred in his face that the chief noticed it, and at length everyone else in the council chamber also did. But none of them asked Gadoh why he did not speak, because such a question was not asked aloud.

The boy had a name and he was glad. Now he would be like other boys of the village. His father spoke again. "This name is long and will be used only at feasts and important occasions.

He shall be known commonly as Rimau (Tiger)."

So the feast ended. The people scattered to their homes, and the boy Rimau retired to his sleeping mat. But as he fell asleep, his last thought was of the furious face of the witch doctor.

4.
Secret Curse

IT WAS SIX DAYS AFTER THE GREAT FEAST. MOST
of the villagers were feeling the effects of the *chachar* medicine.
Many of them were feverish and ill, and few persons were in the
village streets. Chief Feermin had gone to the market village.
Rimau remembered that this was the season for *salak* fruit and
decided to go into the jungle and find some. His mother and the
little girls were hot and uncomfortable from the fever. The sour
sweetness of the *salak* fruit would refresh them.

Taking a soft bag woven of water grass with him, he left the
village and walked in the direction of a deep ravine that cut
through the hills some distance back of the village. He rejoiced
that he had already received his magic mark and now did not
have the fever and the sore arm.

Early in the afternoon he entered the ravine, walking slowly
and softly. He knew that it was always wise to walk quietly in
the jungle, where you could never know what forest creatures
might be about. He heard a faint sound. It came from deep
in the ravine and sounded like a human voice, singing. He
stopped and listened, but the sound had stopped. Then it came
again. Rimau felt no fear, only curiosity. He crept with cau-
tious, catlike steps through the brush under the trees. Guided
by the snatches of weird song, he came to a dense tangle of
vines. He lifted his hands, slowly parted the leafy screen, and

looked down on Gadoh!

The witch doctor was kneeling on a mat. He was shaving thin strips from a bone and laying them beside some small bundles of hair and sticks. Rimau realized that this must be the secret place where Gadoh prepared his devil medicine. Even as he watched, the witch man threw back his head and lifted his voice in a queer, high-pitched song. He was calling the evil spirits, and Rimau knew that he should not be in this place; this was where Gadoh met the spirits and mixed their curses with his devil medicine. Rimau told himself that he should leave at once, but the scene fascinated him. The witch doctor's eyes were glassy and seemed to be fixed on something far away. Although he sat facing a wall of green vines that shut him in on every side, he seemed to be staring into limitless space.

Gadoh gave the peculiar spirit call at frequent intervals. Then at last, with a shudder of delight, he leaned forward over the piles of medicine and gathered them into a little grass bag. Before he tied the mouth of the bag together, he blew into it. Then he uttered the most terrible curse of all: *"Koosta! Koosta!"* After this, he named the name of his victim. "The son of Chief Feermin of the Mamoras—called Rimau!"

The boy could hardly suppress the gasp of horror that rose to his lips. As he drew back into the tangle of vines, where he could no longer see the witch doctor, he was not sure whether he had made a sound or not. Perhaps Gadoh had seen him! He might even now be gathering up his medicines, his mat, and his charms. In another minute he might come rushing after him.

The boy slithered through the brush of the ravine, avoiding the trail by which he had come. He knew now that it was Gadoh's path. When he finally reached the open ground he flew along faster and faster, streaking toward the village and his father's house. He leaped over fallen logs and in one place, where a single pole bridged a creek, he glided along the slender bridge like the tiger for which he had been named. Surely, he thought, Gadoh could not run so fast. He could reach the village before the witch doctor—long before. But what to do then?

Rimau knew that his father would not be home yet. And there was no telling what Gadoh might do if he had seen someone watching him at his devil magic—especially someone whom he had been in the act of cursing.

As Rimau's mind occupied itself with these thoughts, his feet gathered speed. He rushed, panting, into the shadow under his father's house, holding his hand on his chest to still the pounding of his heart. His breath came in short gasps. He remained in hiding among the rubbish there for a minute, until he recovered a little; then he peered all about. He searched the street in every direction. It was deserted; most of the people were inside their houses, sick from the *chachar* medicine. No one had seen him arrive in such terrified haste. That was good. He leaned against a pole and waited for another minute.

Then he began to think more coolly. Surely this was the very place where the witch doctor would look for him first. He could not stay here. Nor could he run to his mother. She would be even more frightened of the witch doctor than he was. He peered out and studied the clumps of trees and bamboo that bordered the village clearing. Then he loosened his green-and-yellow plaid sarong, twisted it tightly around his waist again, and settled his green velvet cap on his head. Finally he came out from under the house and looked around again. He must not act frightened. He must be calm.

Walking away from the great house, he headed for a clump of giant bamboo. As he walked he drew out his sharp belt knife. He wanted the village folk to think he was on his way to cut a length of bamboo for his mother, so he swung the knife and hummed a tune to himself. When he reached the clump of bamboo, he scrambled into the very heart of it, by means of a little path that had been cut by people in search of bamboo joints.

Deep among the huge poles of bamboo he could not be seen. His green-and-yellow sarong blended perfectly with the colors of the bamboo. The old stalks were yellow, with withering leaves of the same shade. The fresh young shoots were bright green. He unfastened his sarong again and nervously tightened it about his waist. Then he squatted down among the humped-up roots and tried to collect his thoughts, to decide what could be done. As he considered the matter, his terror grew. He remembered that in the past almost all the curses of Gadoh had been fulfilled: madness here; lameness there; a feebleminded girl in one house; in another, a grown man become foolish and simple like a little child.

Noone in the village respected the curses of Gadoh more than the chief's son did. And now a curse was being prepared for him! *"Koosta! Koosta* (leprosy)!" That was what Gadoh had said! Rimau felt as though he might die then and there among the bamboo shoots, so great was his terror of the *koosta*.

Someone in the village was shouting. It was Gadoh. "Rimau! Rimau!" he called.

The boy shrank deeper into the thicket and crouched lower among the friendly roots. The bamboo was so thick that he could see nothing outside it, but he kept his ears alert for every sound in the village. He knew that people must be passing back and forth. Now the night came down, and the stars began to come out, one by one. Mosquitoes swarmed around his head. He fought them off with his rajah scarf and finally wrapped it around his head and shoulders.

What sound was this? It was the voice of his father, the chief, who must have returned from the market place. The time had come when Rimau must leave his hiding place and return to his home. It could very well be that Gadoh waited for him there, but he must go. He must tell his father what had happened. Stealing softly through the early darkness, he crept through the village, keeping in the shadows until, at last, he climbed the ladder under his house and stood before Chief Feermin.

The chief took him by the arm. "Where have you been? Your mother is sick from the *chachar* medicine, and you should not have run off like this when I was away. You should have stayed where you could help her. She has been troubled about you all afternoon." The hand grasping his arm tightened and shook him a little.

Rimau tried to speak, but his voice failed him. His throat ached; his heart pounded in his chest. The chief turned him around so that the light from the oil lamp fell on his face. Then he laid a hand on each of his son's shoulders. "Are you sick?" he demanded.

Still the boy could not say anything. There were so many feelings struggling inside him that when a word was almost on his lips another got in its way.

Then Rimau saw his father's face change. Now Chief Feermin was frightened. He made the boy sit down on a mat and began to rub his arms and legs and back. "Did you have a chill?" he asked, in a voice of great tenderness.

Hearing the kindness in his father's voice, something loosened inside Rimau, and he found that he could swallow the big lump in his throat. He opened his mouth. "It is Gadoh!" he croaked, in a voice so harsh and hollow that it sounded strange to him. "Gadoh is making the curse against me—the curse of *koosta!*"

The chief's body jerked to an upright position.

His face was pale. His voice snapped like dry cane in the wind, as he asked, "When did you find out about this?"

"I saw him in his secret place in the ravine. He was preparing a curse. He spoke my name! I know it is against me!"

The chief sank down on the mat beside the boy. He looked old and tired. Then his face grew stern. "Gadoh has been planning this ever since the men brought the *chachar* medicine. He will take great care to make his curse strong and terrible!" The chief bowed his head and clutched it in his hands. There was no sound in the quiet room except the heavy breathing of the frightened boy.

Suddenly Chief Feermin sprang up and jerked Rimau to his feet. "The curse has not yet been laid! Surely it has not yet been laid against this house!" He spoke in a loud, excited voice. "There is still time for you to escape! He will not bring the devil magic and dig the hole near this house until the moon rises! He will wait till we are all asleep." The chief danced about the room in his agitation. He pulled Rimau along with him. 'If you are gone—if you are not in this house-then you will not be harmed. Gadoh's curse will come to nothing!"

35

"But where shall I go?" Rimau felt a terrible fear rising within him again. "It is night. The tigers are about! Where shall I go?"

"My son"—the chief spoke more calmly now—"no tiger is so dangerous as this man Gadoh, once he has set out to destroy you. I never dreamed he would dare to do such a thing!" He patted the boy's arm. "Come. I will take you to the river. We will stay there till morning. Then you must go on, and I will return here."

Rimau bowed his head. Clearly there was no other way. Because the matter was urgent, they went to tell his mother, whose face was still flushed with fever. Even by the faint light of the oil lamp in the bedroom, Rimau could see it. She sat by the two little girls. They tossed and moaned in their sleep, and she watched them with great care, lest they brush their sore arms against the blanket.

"We must send our son away!" The chief whispered, to avoid awakening the sleeping babies.

The chief's wife looked up at him, her eyes big with hurt and surprise; she did not understand. She stood up and followed them into the other room, from which the ladder led to the ground beneath the house. Her long black hair fell to her knees. She was ill and frightened, and as she stood there, her shoulders drooping, she looked no taller than Rimau. "Now tell me what you mean." She gazed at her husband. "It is night. Where will you send the boy in the night?"

The chief looked down at her and spoke slowly, each word falling heavily from his lips. "Gadoh is angry, because I brought the *chachar* medicine to this village against his advice. He thinks I have shamed and belittled him in the eyes of all the village. Now he has prepared a curse against our son. Tonight it will be placed against this house and against this boy!"

The boy's mother put her hand to her head. Rimau knew it must be aching from the fever. When she spoke, her voice was so low that they both bent to listen. "Will sending him away do any good?" she asked.

"Yes." The chief spoke quickly. "The curse has been spoken

and joined with his name, but it will not hurt anyone else, and it will not hurt Rimau if he is not here when it is buried."

"Then he must go!" she said in a stronger voice. "Send him to Ankola. My brother Jimat is there, you remember—he who went to Padang to be a soldier. He is the medicine man for Bitter Valley Village in the Ankola district." She looked at Rimau, and the boy thought he would always remember her like this, with her long black hair hanging loose and her eyes clouded with pain. "When Gadoh's anger is past, we will bring him back again," she said.

"Yes, that is what we will do!" the chief said, beginning to brighten a little. "You are a man already, my son," he added, placing his hand on the boy's shoulder, "and you have the magic of the tigers in your blood. You will not find it difficult to travel from one village to another. You must not carry anything but your belt knife. You will need to hurry and you must have no burden to hinder you. When you get to Bitter Valley, ask for their witch doctor. That will be your uncle—Jimat."

"The boy must wear this same green-and-yellow sarong. It is new and strong," Rimau's mother said. "He must take a new, thick rajah cloth. It will keep him warm at night and it will show everyone that he is the son of a Mamora chief."

Before they started down the ladder, the chief gave his moneybag to the boy. "There is enough here to buy you food for many days," he told him. "It must never be said that the son of a Mamora chief must beg for rice."

After taking one last look at his little sisters, asleep on their mat, the boy left his father's house. His mother came down the ladder, but she said nothing more and she did not cry. She was the wife of a Mamora chief.

As Rimau and his father passed along a back street of the village, they looked toward the witch doctor's house, but they could hear no sound and see no light. Like the other houses, it was dark and quiet. They walked slowly and with great caution until they passed the boundaries of the village; then they hastened along the path and talked without fear.

"He will not find out that you are gone until tomorrow. You

37

must hurry. You must travel away from the lake and cross the mountains to the south." The chief was still thinking about Gadoh.

The path toward the river was much traveled, and therefore broad. There was no danger of losing the way. They walked at a brisk pace, but it was after midnight when they came to the river. A crude bridge of two logs, with a bamboo reed lashed alongside for a handrail, spanned the swift water. Together they crossed it in the darkness. The water cascading over the rocks below made so much noise that they had to speak loudly to be heard.

Once safe across the river, they stopped and rested. They sat on a log where they could watch the bridge and see anyone who crossed it.

"It is possible that Gadoh never saw you at all," the chief said. "He may think that no one knows of his plan. Even now he may be creeping toward our house to dig a hole and lay the devil medicine." They both shuddered.

"Perhaps he didn't see me," Rimau said at last. "Perhaps it was my own surprise and fear that made me think he saw me. But I did hear him call my name when I was hiding in the bamboo."

When the first promise of dawn reddened the hills, they rose from the log where they had been sitting and stood close together for a moment in the fading darkness.

At last Rimau spoke. "My father, I will go now."

"Go in peace, my son."

"Stay in peace, my father."

So they parted, there by the bridge, and Chief Feermin waited, watching Rimau as he turned to the left along the bank of the river, heading toward the mountains that lay to the south. Beyond them was the district of Ankola. The boy did not look back, for there was a fierce urgency in him. With his knife at his belt and the bag of coins fastened under his green-and-yellow sarong, the son of Chief Feermin went forth into the morning toward the unknown jungle and his great adventure.

5.
Night on the Mountain

RIMAU WALKED ALL THAT DAY AND CAME TO A village far from the river. He spent ' only one night there and told no one where he came from. It was not unusual for young men to wander about through the villages. Few people questioned him beyond the usual greeting given to all traveling people: "Where do you go?"

If anyone asked him about his village or family, he explained that he was a wandering boy. "I wish to learn the customs of the different villages," he said. "I am not afraid of the mountains or the jungle."

Some of the old men who spoke to him said it was a brave thing for so young a lad to go out to see the world, but the women shook their heads. Does he have a mother, they wondered. Rimau knew that no Battak walks alone if he has a friend, but he had no friend—not on this Journey.

He had wrapped his rajah scarf in a banana leaf and he took it out only at night. He wanted no one to see that he was the son of a great Mamora chief. He wished only to be unnoticed and unknown until he passed the boundaries of the Toba country.

His father and his home were always in his thoughts. Now the family would be eating. Now his father would be going to the rice field. Now his mother would be pounding out the rice, and his little sisters would be playing on the floor of the kitchen room in the great old house. He could see them all clearly, they seemed so close. As he walked dreamily along, he often felt that he might wake up any minute and find himself on his mat at home.

Then, with a great effort, he would put these thoughts from his mind. I am a man now, he thought to himself. I am able to walk with courage in strange villages and in the jungle. I am thirteen years old. Then he would walk faster and hold his head higher for a little while.

After many days he crossed the mountains that divided Toba from Ankola. Now he wore his rajah scarf openly. The scarf was decorated with heavy beadwork, and fringes bordered both ends. Because it was richly colored and had a special kind of beaded design, anyone he met could see that Rimau was the son of a chief. In his own country of Toba the village people would have known that he was a prince of the Mamora tribe; in Ankola they would see only that he was the son of a Toba chief.

Rimau went from village to village, spending a few days in each, then pressing on farther into the Ankola district. He inquired always about the path to the city of Sipirok, because he knew that the village of Bitter Valley lay on this side of it.

"How far is it to Sipirok?" he asked two men he met one day. They were leading their heavily laden ponies along the trail.

"Two days from here," they told him. "But if you take the short cut across that mountain over there, it is not so far. You might make it in one day."

Rimau thanked them, and taking the short cut, he climbed to a ridge of the mountain they had pointed out to him. He looked down on a grassy slope, with tall jungle growth on either side of it. He knew that this was a place that had been burned over for a rice field a few years back and had not yet sprouted new trees. Probably it never would; the *lalang* grass had taken it over.

40

It was noon when Rimau looked down on the field of *lalang* grass. From the mountain ridge it had looked small-a space that one might cross in an hour. But he stood in the midst of it, and the sinking sun cast a red glow along the mountain to the west. The boy had thrust and torn his way through the tall grass, which was higher than his head and thick, like growing rice. A drenching shower passing up the valley had caught him in the dense, clinging grass. He was soaked to the skin, and the wet blades of the *lalang* had scratched him.

Rimau rested now in an open spot, where a small stream trickled around an outcropping of rocks. Green hummocks of moss rose above the moist earth.

Suddenly he raised his head. Had something moved? What had made that swishing sound, he wondered. He cupped his hand to his ear. It must be the drift of the wind in the *lalang* surely nothing more! He was certain that he was alone in the field of grass. Then he saw the tracks—two of them—almost at his feet. Tiger tracks! Huge ones! He stooped, intending to measure the footprints with his hand; but even as he was reaching toward the nearest one, he saw the moss and tiny ferns that had been crushed by the tiger's paws slowly unbending and straightening.

With a flash of fear the boy looked all around him, expecting to see a pair of fierce eyes glaring from the long grass, or possibly the twitching of a thick, striped tail. The tiger must have passed by only a moment ago! For an instant he stood as still as the rock beside him. Rimau's keen glance darted in every direction. Then slowly he lifted his hand and drew out his belt knife. Rimau was a strong boy of thirteen, and tall for his age. Having spent his whole life in a jungle village, he was accustomed to tigers and knew something about their habits. He knew that even a strong man would have little chance of stabbing a tiger, with only a belt knife for a weapon. It would be almost impossible, unless the tiger was standing directly over him. Rimau had no intention of getting himself into such a position, but he knew that tigers and other savage beasts

41

can often be frightened and driven away by a show of bravery and a loud noise. He felt better with the knife in his hand. If he had discovered the tiger lurking in the *lalang*, he would certainly have charged at him with the knife, screaming all the bad names a Battak boy could think of.

But he couldn't see the tiger; it must have passed on down the mountain. He relaxed a little and leaned against one of the rocks, letting the cool water of the stream wash his tired feet.

The boy still wore his sarong of yellow-and-green plaid. He had pulled it between his legs and fastened it at his waist in front, so he could move more freely through the long grass. Now he loosened the sarong and let it fall like a skirt around his legs. It was wet, and it flapped in the damp wind. Across his shoulder was his rajah scarf and on his head the green velvet cap. Although the cap was wet through, it was still tilted at a rakish angle, like a valiant little boat riding out heavy weather in a rough sea.

Now what shall I do? he asked himself. I don't want to go on through that *lalang*, where the tiger is hiding; and besides, it's getting dark.

Rimau was hungry and tired. At the foot of this mountain lay the village of Bitter Valley, toward which he was journeying. He thought of the thatched Ankola houses on their tall stilts. They were small and frail compared to the great, heavy houses of his own district, but they were safe. He thought of the warm flicker of coconut-oil lamps, the fragrance of fresh-cooked rice. He had not yet seen Bitter Valley, but he knew it would be like the other villages of Ankola through which he had passed. He thought of it with pleasure. He wondered about Jimat. Would his uncle be glad to see him? Was he a cruel and angry man like Gadoh, back in his own Toba village? A wave of longing for his father swept over Rimau. The hollow feeling in his empty stomach was almost painful.

He examined the rocks. The highest one was level with his shoulder. It would be no protection against the tiger, but it was wide and flat, and still warm from the heat of the sun that had shone fiercely on it earlier in the day. Even the shower had not cooled it. He clambered up on the rock, took off his wet garments, and spread them out to dry. Then he stretched the entire length of his body against the warm surface of the rock, lying so that he could see over the edge. He held his belt knife in his right hand.

The night was filled with the hum and buzz of insects and the calls of night birds. Rimau's ears could catch no other sound, although he listened with the keen hearing of a jungle hunter. For an hour he watched and listened, expecting at any moment to see gleaming eyes in the dark and hear the harsh roar of the great cat.

All at once, far down the mountain, he heard sounds of thrashing and bleating-then silence. The tiger must have passed through the *lalang* and surprised a water buffalo. Now he would be feasting—filling his ravenous maw with rich flesh and fresh blood. He would gorge himself and then creep back into the long, thick grass to sleep. This tiger, thought Rimau, may have been living here in the field of *lalang* for a long time. It would be almost impossible to hunt him out. Rimau thought of the village of Bitter Valley. Was it their buffalo that the tiger had killed? It must be. Had he killed others?

The boy lay on the rock and considered what might be done to rid the mountain of such an unwelcome guest. He remembered how his father had speared the tiger that had stolen a water buffalo from Rocky Hills Village. The men had stuffed the tiger's skin with grass and brought it into the village on a long pole. Everyone had cheered and shouted and praised the chief, and they had scoffed and mocked the tiger, which was now nothing but a stuffed skin.

Rimau felt his clothes. They had dried a little, and he put on his sarong and secured his moneybag. Then he threw the thick rajah scarf over his shoulders and spent the rest of the night huddled on the rock.

When morning came, he decided to follow the course of the stream down the mountain. Though less direct, this way was more open and led diagonally away from the spot where he had heard the sounds of the struggle last evening. The going was difficult, but the boy's feet were tough, and he was hungry. He picked a few berries from the bushes along the path, but they did not satisfy his craving for food. He walked faster.

At the foot of the mountain the rice fields began. Rimau walked along their edges until he finally came to the main path that led to the village.

"Where do you go?" people asked him, as they hurried by on their way to work in the fields of growing rice.

"I go to Bitter Valley," he answered each one.

Because of a little hill, it was not possible to see the village until one was actually entering it. The path was cut into the hillside. To the left of the path was a steep, high bank. On the right, toward the main part of the village, the hillside fell away sharply to a little mountain river. The path curved around the hill, following the river, but always above it. As Rimau came to the last sharp rise in the path, he saw the village on his right—a group of thatched houses, clustered on the floor of a tiny mountain valley.

Rimau crossed the rushing river on a wide, flat plank bridge. To his left, where the river cascaded down toward the bridge, was a house standing by itself. It was larger than most of the huts on the other side of the bridge, and Rimau decided it must be the house of the chief. He walked fast, and in a moment he was standing before it.

"*Amang! Amang!*" he called—the word for *father* in the Battak language. The door opened, and a pleasant-looking woman asked him, "What do you want here?"

"I have traveled far, Mother," Rimau said, "and I am hungry. I ask your kind permission to rest a while in your village."

"Come in peace," she said, and opened the door wide. She made him sit down on a mat. Then she brought him a plate of fresh-cooked rice, together with vegetables prepared in coconut cream, and some dried fish. He ate as if he were starved. "It tastes good," he said, smiling at the woman.

She left him for a moment and returned with her little girl. As she sat watching him eat and questioning him about his journey, she looked with interest at his rajah scarf.

Rimau knew that she could tell by the scarf that he was the son of a Toba chief. After answering all her questions politely, he said, "I have come to this village to look for my uncle—Jimat."

"Oh, that's too bad!" she said. "Jimat is not here. He went to Padang Lawas about a month ago, to see about getting some cattle for this village."

"Will he return soon, do you think?" Rimau felt the friendliness of the woman surrounding him like a warm breath of air.

"Of course he will return," she said, running her fingers through the baby's curls. "He will certainly return, but no one can say when. Even if he has already bought the cattle, it will take a long time to drive them from Padang Lawas."

"And the chief?" Rimau asked. "Is he away too?" "He went to the rice field this morning. He will come back before sundown." She regarded Rimau with motherly concern. "When you have finished eating you must go to the spring to bathe. I will show you the way. I will give you an old sarong to put on, so that you can wash this one."

The boy's heart grew warm, but in spite of the woman's kindness, he found himself becoming more and more intent upon the baby girl, who sat in her mother's arms, playing with a tiny green coconut. She was a small child—perhaps three years old.

"Her name is Madoo (Honey)," the chief's wife told him, when she saw that he admired her baby. The child's eyes were large and dark and looked as soft as velvet. Her hair hung in thick black curls about her face; and her skin, a delicate shade of dusky rose, glowed like the petals of a mountain Hower. Her unclothed body was plump and well formed.

Little Madoo took an instant fancy to Rimau. As she made friends with him, smiling shyly, he was reminded of his own little sisters. The older one was just about this size. Pushing away his empty plate, he caught the little girl up in his arms. Then he stood up and swung her to a perch on his shoulder. She laughed with delight and twisted his green velvet cap around until it dangled over one ear.

"She has a big brother who is about your age and size," the woman said. "That is why she likes you so much. You remind her of Paksa. He is with his father at the rice field."

Again Rimau felt a wave of warm satisfaction flow over him. He had eaten and rested. He had found a kind friend and he had played merrily with Madoo. Now the chief's wife showed him the spring; and when he returned from his refreshing bath, she gave him a mat and a mosquito net and told him to rest. Although the day was still young, the boy was tired from his long journey through the mountains, and he gladly obeyed her. With a feeling of contentment that he had not known for many days, he drew his rajah scarf about him and fell asleep.

6.
Tiger Trap

RIMAU SLEPT TILL LATE AFTERNOON. WHEN HE awoke, he sat up on the mat, rubbed his eyes, and wondered where he was. Then he remembered. He was in the chief's house in Bitter Valley Village. It was near sundown, and the men would be coming home from work soon. He decided to go outside and have a look around the place.

As he stood in front of the chief's door he saw that the village lay between two mountains. On the slope of the mountain toward the north grew the field of *lalang* grass where he had found the tiger tracks last night. The rice fields were in that direction. Toward the south was a higher mountain. Most of the village huts faced in that direction. The lower slope of this mountain was not steep, and on it the boy could see coffee gardens and a few plantings of vegetables.

He lifted his eyes to the higher slopes. Halfway to the summit of the southern mountain he saw a fresh clearing and wondered why it had been made. It was a long way from the village.

A peculiar object on the mountain caught the boy's attention. It was a tremendous rock-more like a jagged hill of rock, in fact. Perched at a dangerous angle, it looked as if it had been thrown at the mountain and was lodged there temporarily. Heavy jungle growth covered its lower crags but could not conceal the severity of its outlines. The top looked like a knife, with its cutting edge turned toward the sky. On the side that Rimau could see, the rock fell away in a precipice from the straight knifelike edge. He could not guess its height but supposed it might be several hundred feet. Rimau regarded the rock with a fascination he could not explain. He wondered if anyone had ever climbed to the top of it.

Now he heard a babble of voices. The men were returning from the rice fields, and they talked in loud, excited voices as they crossed the Hat bridge into the village. "It is Toko-Batoo's buffalo this time," they shouted. "The tiger killed it last night and fed upon it!"

People came running out of the houses and gathered around the men, eager to hear the news. They were filled with consternation as they talked about this latest damage the tiger had done. No one paid any attention to Rimau except little Madoo, who came shyly out of the house and hung onto his hand as he stood close to the wall of the chief's big thatched hut.

"This makes six buffalo!" one of the villagers said. Rimau knew he was the chief, because of his rich scarf and pleated turban.

"Ten goats and one pony have also been taken," another man added.

One of the women spoke up. "Soon we shall have no animals left."

The chief was a strong, stocky man of about forty. The hair showing beneath his turban was thick and curly. His jaws were heavy; his chin jutted out. His beautiful black scarf was decorated with red beads, and he wore it with a jaunty air. He moved with a deerlike grace and sureness, like a man accustomed to following the steep mountain paths. His eyes were black and piercing; his look was stern. Rimau remembered his father's face. The look was the same look a chief of the Battak people must have. There was power in this man—a quiet kind of authority.

The Tiger of Bitter Valley

Rimau touched the nearest man on the shoulder. "I am newly come to your village. Tell me, what is the name of your chief?"

The man turned and looked the boy over with a calculating stare. "His name is Sutan Dolok, which means King of the Mountains." He pointed to a well-built youngster standing close to the chief. "That is the chief's only son, Paksa."

Now the chief spoke. "This tiger has been living in the field of *lalang* for a month," he said in a strong voice. "We can't hunt him out. The field is too large. It is too dangerous to burn so large a field of grass. We must think of some way to trap the tiger." The men pressed close around the chief. They described all the places where they had seen the tiger's footprints. None of them had seen the tiger. Lifting Madoo in his arms, Rimau joined the group around the chief. "It's a great pity Jimat is away," one of the men said. Rimau soon learned that he was Toko-Batoo, whose buffalo had been killed last night. "It was just after Jimat left that the tiger came," said another man. Rimau turned and looked at him. He was a small fellow, with a thin face and a pointed chin. A few coarse black whiskers bristled around his small mouth. When he spoke he lifted his chin and formed his lips into a circle. There was a whine in his voice, and the words came out in a moist splutter.

Rimau nudged the man next to him again. "Who is that fellow?" he asked.

"Teekoos," the man answered, with a nervous laugh. "Teekoos—the Rat!"

Rimau studied the little man's face. With those sharp whiskers and that little round mouth, the poor fellow certainly looked something like a rat.

The men were still speaking about Jimat. Some of them seemed inclined to think that the presence of the tiger near Bitter Valley was due to his being away.

The chief looked at them sternly. "It is useless to blame Jimat," he said. "I sent him after those cattle, and when he has found them he will return. We ourselves must take care of

50

this tiger, and we must do it now, or we shall have no animals left. Let us talk this over."

So the men squatted down on the path near the chief's door. They were tired after their day's work, and they rolled quids of betel nut and chewed while they rested. The older men described different kinds of traps they had seen.

Someone suggested that all the animals had better be tethered in the village at night. Toko-Batoo objected. "The first buffalo the tiger took was tied right beside my house!"

At last they decided to dig a deep pit and cover it with bamboo reeds and earth, hoping that the tiger would fall into it. It was a whole day now since the tiger had killed Toko-Batoo's buffalo.

Rimau stepped forward, still holding Madoo in his arms. "Chief Sutan Dolok," he began respectfully, "I was traveling toward this village last night, but the darkness overtook me on yonder mountain." He pointed to the north. "I was close to the outcropping of rocks in the middle of the *lalang*, where the stream divides it. There I saw the tracks of the tiger. A little later I heard the cry of the water buffalo, as he killed it. That was early in the evening."

The chief looked at Rimau searchingly. "You are from Toba?" he asked, glancing at his rajah scarf.

"I am from Toba," the boy answered.

"Do you have tiger magic in your villages in Toba?" the chief asked him. At this the grim faces of the men relaxed a little. Some of them even smiled.

"We have our spears," the boy replied, and the men laughed.

The villagers knew that the tiger would return to his kill tonight, but now the sun was setting, and there was no time to dig the pit. No one could be sure he would come back to the kill a third time.

"I think we shall have to use a goat when we dig the pit tomorrow," the chief said. "We can tie it out on the mountain. The tiger will hear it cry and he will come for it. Then he will fall into the trap."

Rimau studied Paksa, the chief's son. He was stocky, like his father, but he had the friendly ways of his mother. He wore a red sarong and a red velvet cap. Several times Rimau had discovered Paksa's eyes fixed on him. Now he edged closer to him, and finally stood at his side.

"Who are you?" Paksa asked. "I have the same name as your enemy." Rimau laughed. "The tiger?" The boy laughed too. "Your name is Rimau?"

"You guess well."

"Why did you come here?"

"I came to visit my uncle—Jimat," Rimau said. "He is my mother's brother."

The boys were interrupted by the sound of the chief's voice. He was announcing that six men of the village would go out early the following morning to prepare the trap for the tiger.

After this the crowd began to scatter. Chief Sutan Dolok came over to the boys and laid his hand on Rimau's shoulder. "Why have you come here?" he asked.

Rimau told him, and the chief looked steadily into his eyes. "You may stay in my house tonight," he said.

"I would like to go with the men to dig the tiger trap tomorrow," said Rimau.

"If you are willing to dig and carry dirt you may go," the chief told him.

"I would like to go too," said Paksa.

Rimau saw the look of deep affection that Sutan Dolok gave his son, and as he remembered his own father, a lump rose in his throat.

After some hesitation the chief answered Paksa. "You may go," he said, and the boy's face lit up with great happiness.

Rimau spent the evening talking with Paksa and playing with Madoo. He also thought a great deal about home, and it seemed to him that he had never been able to see it so clearly in his mind before.

Next morning, as they hurried along the path between the rice fields, the boys walked with Toko-Batoo. Rimau pointed to the southern mountain. "What is the reason for that clearing, high on the mountainside?" he asked.

"It is for coffee plants," Toko-Batoo said. "The earth is very good in that spot. As soon as we catch the tiger we can plant the coffee. We have the plants ready. Pretty soon they will spoil, and they are costly." "What has the tiger got to do with the coffee plants?" Rimau asked.

"The people are afraid of the tiger," Paksa told him. "They think the tiger will come to eat them if they go out on the mountain."

Rimau looked at the mountain again. "That big rock"—he pointed to the giant mass of stone that had attracted his attention the night before—"what is that?"

Toko-Batoo grinned. "It is a small mountain of rock, solid rock. What else would it be?" "It looks so strange, as if someone had thrown it there. But of course no one did."

"I should say not!" Toko-Batoo laughed. "It doesn't look so big from here, but it is enormous. To walk around the base of it would take almost an entire day."

"I should like to climb it," Rimau said. Toko-Batoo looked frightened. "No one has ever done that. It is the home of evil spirits.

Its name is Nangir-Jati. Stay away from it! You will get hurt if you go there!" Toko-Batoo hurried along the path and Rimau knew that he did not want to talk about Nangir-Jati any more.

The men did not go to the place where Toko-Batoo's buffalo had been killed and eaten. They walked along a grassy slope near the rice fields, where the little stream trickled down the mountain. There they selected a spot for the pit. Some of the men dug, while the others carried the dirt away. They changed places often, and the work went forward steadily. When the pit began to get deep, they drew up baskets of dirt with rattan thongs. Then they carried all the dirt to the other side of the little stream. It would never do, they knew, to leave a pile of fresh earth near the hole. The tiger might suspect a trap if he saw or smelled anything unusual.

53

The Tiger of Bitter Valley

It took a long time to dig the hole, although the earth was moist and there were no stones. Only the tree roots interfered with the digging. The two boys worked hard carrying dirt.

"Make it narrow and deep! Make it deep ... deep!" Toko-Batoo kept shouting to the men. He was the one in charge of the digging. "It must be so deep that even the largest tiger can't spring out, and it must be so narrow at the bottom that he can't turn around."

By evening the trap was finished. It was about fourteen feet deep and four feet across at the top, but it was narrower at the bottom. Light strips of bamboo were laid across the hole. On top of them the men scattered dirt, handful by and leaves on top of the dirt, so that it would look like the rest of the ground. Finally he tied the goat right beside the trap, and placed two big logs in such a position that the tiger would have to cross the trap to get at the goat. This done, everyone started back to the village, hoping that their enemy would be deceived and fall into the pit they had prepared for him.

On the way home Rimau remembered that today he must find some other place in the village where he might stay. It was a polite custom for the chief to entertain visitors for a night, but Rimau knew that for longer periods one should make other arrangements.

Rimau looked at Toko-Batoo. He had a kind face, and although he was still a young man his shoulders were stooped, as though he had dug many pits and carried many heavy loads. His black velvet cap, which he wore constantly, had a little red feather in it.

"How many folk live in your house?" the boy inquired. "Just my wife and I." Toko-Batoo looked at Rimau closely. "Why do you ask?"

"I should like to stay at your house until my uncle, Jimat, comes back," Rimau said. "Will you allow me to stay there?"

"Are you planning to become a witch doctor, like your uncle?" asked Toko-Batoo.

Rimau had never thought of such a thing. He had always known that someday he would be chief of Rocky Hills Village-though now he could no longer be sure of this. Did witch doctors ever become chiefs, he wondered. "I should like to study magic," he said finally. "But I don't think I could be a witch doctor." "Maybe your uncle will teach you." Toko-Batoo smiled. "Anyway, you are welcome to stay with us till he comes back." Paksa was sorry that Rimau was going. "I wish you could stay with us always," he said. "That would not be right," said Rimau. "But I shall be only a few doors away. We shall have lots of fun together." That evening, with the chief's permission, the boy went to Toko-Batoo's house. His wife spread a mat for Rimau in a small back room and told him he might have this place for himself. He was invited to eat some of their rice and curry. Then, being very tired, he went to his sleeping mat. But he could not sleep, for he kept thinking of his father and mother and the little girls. There was a small window in Rimau's room. During the night he heard a sound, as if someone had passed under the window—someone with naked feet. Now how can that be, Rimau thought. He knew that it was not the custom of the Battak people to wander about alone at night. No one went anywhere without a friend, if he had one.

The second time he heard the footsteps he crept to the window and looked out. Someone was prowling about among the houses. It looked like a man—a lone figure. Rimau could not make out anything else about him. He passed along through the village in the moonlight, then moved toward the mountain to the south.

Who could it be? Rimau's curiosity was aroused. Could this be a man of Bitter Valley who didn't know about the tiger? The ferocious beast might spring on him at any moment!

The boy went back to his mat; but he lay awake for a long time, thinking about the tiger and worrying about the prowler. Then he wondered what would happen if the trap failed to catch the tiger. Would Uncle Jimat be blamed for that, too?

He twisted and turned on his mat until it was nearly morning. Then he fell into a deep sleep.

"Wake up! Wake up!" Toko-Batoo was calling him in a loud voice. "We are leaving for the tiger trap at once. Come along!"

Rimau scrambled to his feet, and together they joined the other men who had dug the pit yesterday and were now going back to inspect it.

"Where is Paksa?" Rimau asked, as they started down the hill. "The chief never lets his son go where there is danger," Toko-Batoo said.

Along the way the men speculated about what might have happened during the night. Teekoos was one of the company, and he had brought his spear along. "I will kill the tiger!" he told everyone. "It is I, Teekoos, who will spear the tiger in the trap!"

Rimau smiled at his boasting. Teekoos was the smallest of all the men; he was scarcely taller than Rimau. Toko-Batoo saw the boy smiling. "He is very skilled in throwing the spear," Toko Batoo said. "He is good at all kinds of killing."

Rimau felt a little embarrassed and changed the subject. "Tell me," he asked, "is it the custom for the people of Bitter Valley Village to wander around alone in the middle of the night?"

"No, of course not," Toko-Batoo answered. "Because of the tiger, every person must be indoors early, and no one may go out into the village during the night. That is the command of the chief. Why do you ask?"

"I thought I saw someone last night," Rimau said. Then he began to wonder if he had really seen anyone. Surely no one would have disobeyed the chief's order.

"You were probably dreaming about the tiger." Toko-Batoo laughed at him. Rimau decided to say nothing more about the matter. It must have been someone from another village.

They walked on briskly. Everyone was eager to see if the tiger had been caught. As they drew near the trap, no one spoke. They crept up to the spot. Then someone shouted, "The goat is gone! The goat is gone!"

They ran to the trap. The strips of bamboo they had laid over the pit were broken. A sound of snarling came from the direction of the trap. Everyone was certain that the tiger had been caught. At the instant when they were about to look into the pit, a huge tiger burst from the *lalang* grass behind them—not twenty yards away. Teeth bared, snarling in fury, the magnificent beast bounded toward the open pit. The men scattered like kapok fluffs before a gust of wind. Rimau felt his heart pounding with terror. He scrambled up into the branches of the nearest tree, which was the one where the goat had been tied, and hung onto a limb, trembling. Where were all his companions? They had vanished like shadows in the night. He was alone with the tiger. But the great beast took no notice of Rimau and made no effort to overtake any of the men. It stood still, looking down through the broken bamboo strips into the pit, and made a harsh, mewing sound. Then Rimau heard another mew, from below, and knew that there were two tigers.

It must be a mother and her young one, he thought; and it was the young tiger that had fallen into the pit. Now the mother tiger was frantic. Her cub was down in the deep hole.

Rimau tried to collect his wits and think clearly. Here he was, far from the village, sitting in a tree with an angry tigress beneath it. He trembled with fright. There was no chance of the tiger's leaving, because her cub was in the pit. She might stay for days! The village men would certainly not return. They had been terribly frightened. Not one of them would venture back. If they thought of him at all, it would be to suppose that he had been killed by the tiger.

The boy remembered how, on the shores of Lake Toba, a tiger had licked his foot, but left him uninjured. Was it true that he had some magic in his blood that protected him from tigers? He desperately hoped so. If only he could think of some way to help the tiger get her cub out of the pit! Then she would go away. But he couldn't think of any sensible thing to do.

He settled himself in a crotch of the tree, taking great pains

57

not to make any noise. He had no wish to draw the tigress's attention to himself. He thought so hard about his problem that he scarcely noticed the passage of time. Still he couldn't think of any way to help the tigress. She was becoming more and more angry. She padded about the hole, taking care not to go too close. She smashed all the bamboo strips and pushed them into the pit, along with the grass and dirt that had been piled on top of them. Now the edge of the hole could be seen clearly.

Still her fury grew. She clawed and tore at the moist earth. Some of it fell into the hole. Once she almost fell in herself. It was only by clawing wildly at the edge that she managed to get back on solid ground.

Now Rimau could see the young tiger. The dirt and rubbish that the mother tiger had pushed into the pit filled it a bit, so the cub could climb a little higher. It was a male, about half-grown. He looked mean, Rimau thought already a killer.

The sun climbed steadily in the heavens. It was nearly noon. Still the boy crouched in the tree. Would he starve to death here, he wondered. How many days could one live without food? The mother tiger continued her terrible march around the open pit. Each time she clawed her way around it, more dirt fell in. At last the great beast seemed to realize that the hole was getting more shallow. She began pawing like a dog, pushing the soil and rubbish into the pit.

Soon the distance to the cub was only about eight feet. The mother tiger looked into the hole, as if to measure it. Then she jumped in. The young tiger crawled on her back and jumped out easily. The tigress backed and pushed against the sides of the pit, trying to make room for herself to spring.

She gathered herself for a leap, but failed. The cub stood by the pit, whining softly. He seemed to be trying to encourage his mother.

She tried a second time and fell back; but the third time, she gained a foothold. Furiously clawing, scratching, and digging, she drew herself out of the trap. Then she stood still and licked her son. They seemed to hold some kind of communion.

The Tiger of Bitter Valley

After a long time they walked off together through the *lalang*. Their bright orange and black stripes glistened in the last rays of the evening sunlight. Rimau followed the undulations of the long grass with his eyes as far as he could, but it was growing dark now.

He waited until he was sure the tigers were far up the mountain—so far that they could not hear him. Then he got down from the tree, stretched his cramped legs, and set out for the village. There was a half moon, and he could see his way between the fields of wet rice. He was no longer afraid of the tigers. He did not think they would come back to that mountain again for a long time.

7.
Terrible Traveler

AS RIMAU HURRIED THROUGH THE RICE FIELDS ON
his way back to Bitter Valley, he wondered what the people
would say when they saw him coming back, alive and unhurt.
They would certainly be surprised. It would be a good time
to tell them about the tiger magic in his blood. Perhaps then
they would believe that he had driven the tigers away with a
charm. But he remembered Gadoh and his cheating ways and
resolved that he would never be like Gadoh. He would never
pretend anything that was not actually so—never use dishon-
esty to further his own purposes or to make people favor him.

He picked his way among the narrow paths in the moonlight
until he came to the main path. There he stopped and rested a
minute, for he had hurried and was almost out of breath. There
was much to think about. He looked back toward the northern
mountain—the mountain of the tigers; then he turned toward
the peaceful valley where the village nestled. A twinge of lone-
someness caught at his heart. He felt so small a thing in this
great, wild country. He wondered what his father was doing
now.

As Rimau started on again, he came to the little hill in
front of the village, where the path curved upward. He was

61

not thinking of danger. Indeed, he had no idea that danger lurked between him and the safety of his sleeping mat in To-ko-Batoo's house.

All at once he heard a sound, a gurgling sound. He could hear footsteps ahead, just around a bend in the path. They were coming toward him. There was no time to run-no place to hide. Suddenly the boy was afraid. He felt a prickle along his scalp, though he had heard nothing but the footsteps and the peculiar noise.

Rimau knew that a lone traveler was an unusual thing in the Battak land, even by day. And no well-intentioned person wandered alone at night, if he could avoid it. But then he remembered that he was alone. Perhaps this traveler had just as good a reason for walking alone and at night as he had. Still, he could not quiet the hammering of his heart. The steps sounded closer. The gurgling sound was louder.

The pathway was cut into the hill, so that there was a high, steep bank on the left side. On the right, toward the village, the bank fell away to the swift little river. There was no place to hide. He must meet the solitary traveler face to face.

Now a peculiar terror took hold of him. He knew in his heart that only evil men ordinarily walk alone, and the gurgling noise was horrible. He remembered the prowler he had seen from his window last night. A faint nausea stole over him, as though a loathsome odor defiled the night. Yet it was not a smell that disturbed him; it was a sense of terrible danger—a feeling that some deadly evil was coming toward him in the moonlight.

Now the thing came into sight. It was a man, a lone figure, like himself. He was much taller than Rimau, even though his head was hunched forward between his shoulders.

There was no way to avoid this meeting in the narrow path. As the man raised his head, the boy's heart pounded with fright. He stood still and looked into that hideous face, now less than five feet away. Even in the faint light he could see the fierce eyes, which glared at him through a tangle of long hair. The man's mouth was working, but from it issued no

words-only the gurgling sounds.

The man reached out a bony hand and grasped Rimau's shoulder. The boy sprang aside, but the man's strength was enormous. His fingers were hard and rough, and stronger than Rimau would have thought possible. He struggled in that iron grasp, while the man gurgled and laughed—a terrifying sound.

Without words or any other sound, the two battled in the path. They were less than a hundred yards from the first of the village houses. A scream rose in Rimau's throat, but he stifled it. No help could come from the village. If they heard his cry tonight, they would be sure the tiger had eaten him up and that his spirit was returning to haunt them.

No, he must save himself. He flew into a passion of fury. He bit and clawed and twisted, like a fighting cat; but the dreadful grip did not loosen. The madman's hideous laughter and moist chuckling and gurgling continued. Tired now, and hopeless, the boy let himself go limp.

Then the man spoke. "I am hungry," he said. "But I have no food," Rimau gasped, still limp in the man's hands. "I am hungry too."

"Then I will eat you!" The hand on the boy's right shoulder loosened and reached for his throat. With a lightning speed born of his terror, Rimau jerked from the monster's grasp and streaked up the hill, and across the bridge into the village. With the man's feet pounding after him, he hid himself in the shadows under one of the houses and stayed there until he saw the terrible figure stalking some distance away, between the huts.

Then he hurried to Taka-Batao's door and called out in a low voice. It was already late. Taka-Batao might be in bed. But the boy saw a faint light gleaming through a crack in the door. Taka-Batao must be awake inside, sitting on his mat. Rimau called again. Then he heard the voice of Teekoos. Teekoos was sitting this night in Taka-Batao's house, and the two of them must be so busy talking that they did not hear his call. He tried again, this time in so loud a voice that he was afraid the creature he had just escaped would hear him and come back.

Then Taka-Batao unbarred the door. He opened it just a crack and saw who stood outside. He was petrified with surprise and stood where he was in stunned silence without opening the door.

Now Rimau was sure he could hear the sound of naked feet running. He expected at any instant to feel a clawing hand at his throat. He pushed the door open, almost knocking Toko-Batoo down in his haste to get inside. Swiftly he closed the door behind him and pushed the heavy wooden bar securely into place.

Rimau was winded from his wild tussle and the run up the hill. He ran his hand through his hair, for it was standing up like broken rice plants in a wind. He supposed that his face also showed signs of fright and agitation. Rimau did not like to arrive at Toko-Batoo's house in such an undignified manner. It was not becoming to the son of a Mamora chief. And, of course, he had not expected to find Teekoos here. The Rat's eyes showed surprise, and cunning, too.

"Did the tiger chase you all the way to the village?" Toko-Batoo asked, when he had recovered from his surprise.

Rimau waited a moment to get back his breath. Then he glanced at Teekoos, and said,

"The tiger did not chase me. I was in a hurry to get home."

"Then you are not hurt?" Toko-Batoo asked.

"I am not hurt," the boy said. "My father told me that I have the magic of the tigers in my blood. That is why I am called Rimau." He looked at Teekoos again. Rimau sensed something about Teekoos—something he could not name or describe. He felt as if it were Gadoh who sat in Toko-Batoo's house that night.

"But the tiger was coming straight for you," Teekoos said, in his whining voice. "We all saw the tiger!"

"Where is the tiger?" Toko-Batoo demanded.

Rimau spread his arms and flapped them airily, as if to show them that the tiger had taken wings and flown away. "Gone, gone!" he said. "I don't think they will come back to that mountain. There were two tigers—a mother and her cub."

The two men were filled with wonder. Toko-Batoo's wife came out and set rice and curry before the Tiger Boy, as he was often called after that night. He was hungry after his long day in the tree, but thought it best to eat only one plate of rice. His stomach could not bear more that evening.

Rimau resolved to say nothing about his fight on the path as long as Teekoos was present. He felt a growing distrust of this small fellow. The Rat might use the information to do harm or cause trouble. With a great effort, he suppressed his frightening story and went to his sleeping mat, leaving the two men to swap tiger tales.

That night, as he lay on his mat, he reviewed the whole affair. He knew that less than a generation ago the people of his country had practiced cannibalism. The eating of human flesh had been a common occurrence. Rimau considered whether the thing he had met on the path might be an evil spirit which had risen up to revive the old customs. He could not quite believe this. He reached up and felt his shoulder, which still ached from that clutching hand. The creature must have been a living man, for its fingers had felt like iron. How could a man's hands become so hard and strong? Rimau decided only one thing: the man on the road and the prowler he had seen on his first night in Toko-Batoo's house were the same being. He resolved never to go outside the hut again after sundown.

By the time Rimau had eaten breakfast the following morning, the whole village knew that one young boy had driven off two tigers. The story grew as it passed from lip to lip. People said that the men actually had seen Rimau in the tiger's jaws and that her claws were ripping him to pieces. Then, they said, he had used his secret tiger magic, and the beast had become a coward, like a lamb or a sheep. It lost all power to hunt and kill, so that the Tiger Boy had come back without a scratch or a wound.

When Rimau awoke and heard reports of the town gossip, he regretted boasting the night before and not telling the whole story of the tigers. Toko-Batoo was not in the house, and he went to find his friend. "Toko-Batoo," he said, "it is not true that I chased the tigers away. I was as frightened as the rest of you. I was near a tree and I climbed it. From there I saw the tigress rescue her young one from the pit."

"How do you know that your tiger magic didn't make the whole matter work out as it did?" Toko-Batoo smiled.

Rimau thought this over for a moment. "If any tiger magic was working, I didn't know it," he said.

That day a group of villagers were brave enough to go back to the pit. Tracks and marks of the tigress were everywhere. The men came home filled with excitement. How could a young boy have spent a day there with the tigress and escaped without harm?

That day Rimau told Toko-Batoo about his meeting with the man on the path. "Do you know anything about this man?" the boy asked. "Has he ever threatened people before? Who is he?"

"You have asked me hard questions." Toko-Batoo sat on his heels and rubbed the whiskers on his chin. "The chief has forbidden us to talk about this thing."

"What do you mean? I struggled for my life on the road entering this village—and the chief won't allow me to know who it was I met? Why is it such a secret?" Rimau felt anger rising within him.

Toko-Batoo spread his hands in a gesture of apology. "Of course, it is not right. I mean it is not right for you to be the only one who doesn't know. The madman is Kala—the chief's younger brother!"

Rimau caught his breath in surprise. "The chief's brother … the chief's brother?" He sat down facing Toko-Batoo and leaned toward him. "How did he ever get like that?"

"He is several years younger than the chief, and the chief greatly loved him. In fact, he had promoted him to be his chief counselor just before it happened."

"What happened?" Rimau urged him on. "We think the

67

medicine of madness was made against him. The chief grieves all the time for his brother. He doesn't want anyone to mention it."

"When did the madness come?" Rimau asked.

"About two years ago. It came suddenly. Kala had just finished building his new house and had moved his wife and baby into it." Toko-Batoo's eyes were filled with sadness. "One day he went with Teekoos to tend his garden on the southern mountain. Teekoos came back the same day, but Kala stayed away for three days. When he came back, his face was blue and his eyes were wild. He made funny noises with his mouth. He didn't know anyone—not even his wife and baby!" Toko-Batoo looked so tired and grieved that Rimau knew he was deeply troubled. "He was my best friend … my best friend!"

"Was his house in this village?" Rimau asked.

"Yes. It's the only one over on the other side of the village beyond the bridge." "Does someone live there now?" the boy asked. "No one lives there. Evil spirits stay there. Sometimes we hear them crying in the night."

"I suppose Kala comes back to visit his house. Perhaps that is what you hear. How dangerous is he?" The boy remembered the clutching hand on his shoulder. For a moment his mouth felt dry and his breath came faster. The fight on the path was vivid in his mind, as if it had happened but a moment ago. "I have heard stories. People say that during these two years of his madness he has eaten raw flesh. They say he eats frogs and small chickens and other little creatures that are easily captured. About six months ago there was a story told that he ate a boy from a village on the west slope of the mountain." Now Rimau knew that the creature he had met on the path was this madman—Kala. It had not been an evil spirit after all. A deep sadness stole over the man and the boy, as they considered these grave matters. They ate their evening meal in silence.

8.
Mountain Garden

SUTAN DOLAK WAITED FOR A WEEK. THE TIGER did
not come back, and there were no more killings. He sent for
Rimau. "Your medicine is good!" he told the boy. "Will you stay
in this village and help us with your magic?"

Rimau looked down at the ground and fumbled with the
fringe of his scarf. All this talk about tiger magic made him
uneasy. "I don't think it was my magic that drove the tigers
away," he blurted out. "When Uncle Jimat comes back perhaps he will teach me some good magic. But I would like to
stay here, if you are willing."

"It is enough." Sutan Dolok looked pleased. "I know witchcraft when I see it. I know tiger magic when I see it. Will you
go to the mountain gardens with my people? They go to plant
the coffee." His voice was almost pleading. "They are still
afraid of the tigers, and Jimat is not here. But they believe in
your magic. They will go if I send you with them."

Then Rimau thought of the evil creature who prowled the
village by night. He was not afraid of the tigers; they were
probably far away by now. But this man Kala might haunt the
mountain gardens, too. What kind of magic could be used to
protect the people from him?

"Master," he addressed the chief. "It is necessary to plant the coffee, and I will go with the people. But I beg you to send the bravest and strongest men, for there are other dangers beside the tiger."

"What dangers do you fear?" Sutan Dolok drew his black-and-red scarf tightly around his shoulders and looked at Rimau with piercing eyes.

"Evil men are more dangerous than evil beasts," the boy said.

Then the chief turned pale, and anger showed in his face. "Have you met any evil men in this village?"

Rimau looked straight into Sutan Dolok's eyes and took a step toward him. He lowered his voice to a whisper. "I have met a person both cruel and dangerous. I know he is a madman."

Then Sutan Dolok's face lost its anger, and his expression changed to one of deep sadness. Distress clouded his eyes. "You may go now," he said softly.

So Rimau did not tell him of his encounter with Kala.

That night Rimau and Toko-Batoo went to bed early, for the chief had sent word around the village that the coffee planters would leave at an early hour. They would go all the way to the clearing, high on the slope of the southern mountain.

Rimau lay awake for a while, thinking about what he had said to Sutan Dolok. Perhaps he should not have mentioned the madman Kala to the chief. But he was not willing to go with the planters to the coffee garden unless the chief fully realized the dangers they might meet.

It seemed but a moment later when he heard Toko-Batoo calling, "Wake up! Wake up! We are leaving to plant the coffee." Rimau tumbled out from under his mosquito net, and in a few minutes he joined the little group of men and women who were gathered in front of the chief's house. The first rosy flush of morning showed behind the mountains.

"See!" The chief grasped Rimau's arm. "See! I have chosen the strong and the brave of this village to go with you. Take care that they do not come to harm."

The coffee plants were divided among all of them, so that each had a heavy load to carry. Their path led straight from the chief's doorway, past the large open meadow where weekly market was held every Tuesday. Rimau felt relieved when he saw that Teekoos was not one of the chosen company. Something about the Rat disturbed him! But he was sorry that Paksa had not been allowed to go. Rimau liked Paksa and his company would have been pleasant.

When the sun came up the air grew warmer, and the men puffed and sweated as they toiled up the steep trail. It was midmorning when they reached the clearing and set their burdens down. Everyone was tired, but one thought was uppermost in every mind: the plants must be put into the ground as quickly as possible, so that they would not have to spend the night on the mountain.

From the mountain clearing Rimau had a closer view of the great rock, Nangir-Jati. The path they had taken had led them past its base. Now they were above it. As the boy looked down on the sharp angles of the curiously shaped rock, he was once again impressed by its sinister look. He paused for a moment to examine it, wondering if it would be possible for a human being to climb those precipitous heights. As he looked, he thought he saw something move on the sharp ridge at the top of the rock. What could it be? He looked again and was sure there was really something moving on the rock. "Look, there on Nangir-Jati," he called to Toko-Batoo. "Do you see something moving along the ridge on this side?"

Toko-Batoo wiped the sweat from his brow with the back of his hand and shaded his eyes with his arm. "I can't see anything," he said.

Perhaps it was a monkey, Rimau thought. The jungle was full of big monkeys. Every morning at daybreak they filled the whole valley with their musical chatter.

Rimau stopped trying to make out what he had seen. He left the others at their digging and walked in a circle around the edge of the clearing. He had remembered that the chief had sent him along with the planters to protect them while they worked. Although he doubted that he possessed any magic, he felt proud, because the chief trusted him. He could not help thinking how wonderful it would be if he really did have some magic that would kill tigers, make madmen well again, and protect people from injury.

It was not possible to see far into the dense jungle above the clearing, but at the upper end of the coffee garden the boy came upon something that surprised and frightened him—tiger tracks! He stooped down and examined them with care. They looked similar to the ones he had found in the patch of *lalang* on the northern mountain. It must be the same tigress, he thought, but he could not find the claw prints of the young tiger. He was very troubled as he made his way back to the spot where the villagers were working, but he resolved to say nothing about the tiger tracks for the present. It would worry the women. They would want to leave the work undone and return to the village at once. Rimau picked up his heavy grub hoe and began to dig.

All through the day the planters worked hard, hurrying as much as possible. But they had to be careful. The coffee plants were very delicate, and the village had paid a large price for them.

By mid afternoon everyone knew the disappointing truth: they could not possibly finish the work and get back to the village before dark. They would have to spend the night on the mountain, for the trail was too steep and dangerous to travel after nightfall. "We might as well cook the rice," one of the women said. She and her friend had come along to prepare food for the planters. "We will all feel better after we eat," she added. Everyone agreed with her, so the two women made a fireplace of stones in the shade of a crude shelter that had been built long ago. They set a kettle of rice on the fire to boil. While one of them watched the rice, the other went to hunt for vegetables. She came back with an armful of tender shoots from a squash vine, a coconut, and a few tiny squashes, the size of eggs. She washed the vegetables in a mountain spring behind the shelter and put them in a clay pot to boil. Then she grated the coconut with a crude scraper she had brought from the village. When the vegetables were cooked, she poured a rich milk, squeezed from the coconut gratings, over them and took the pot off the fire.

The workers gathered, squatting in the shade of the shelter. They brought young, tender banana leaves with them, and the rice and vegetables were served on the leaves. No forks or spoons were needed; everyone used his fingers. Rimau sat with the others, enjoying the food, but his mind was still troubled.

"We will have to spend the night here," Toko-Batoo said, while they were eating. "We shall scarcely be able to finish the planting by sun-down."

"Where will we sleep?" Rimau asked.

"The best place to sleep would be on the platform of this shelter," said Toko-Batoo, looking up at the raised floor. There was a grass roof over it, but it had no walls. "I think there is room enough for all of us there, if we lie close together," he added.

"But in the night animals may come!" Rimau objected. "We will make a big fire. No animals come where there is a big fire." Then Toko-Batoo looked closely at the boy. "What animals do you fear?"

"Tigers!" the boy said. "I saw the tracks of one up there." He pointed toward the upper edge of the clearing.

Toko-Batoo shifted his position, so that he could see the spot, but he kept on eating. He finished his rice, threw away his banana leaf, and ran his hands through his shock of hair to clean them. Then he put on his black cap, and said, "Come. Show me."

Everyone followed, and they all inspected the footprints with great care and fear.

"These tracks are not very fresh," Toko-Batoo said, after he had bent over them for a long time. "I doubt that the tiger is around here now, and I'm sure no tiger will come near if we make a big fire and keep it burning all night."

The women wanted to forget about the rest of the coffee plants and go home at once, but the men laughed at them. "Didn't the chief say he was choosing only the strong and the brave to come today?" they said proudly.

Now the sun had almost dropped behind the low mountains down the valley, and the little group of workers hurried to finish the last of the planting, while there was still light to see. Before the last plant was in the ground, some of the men began to gather wood. Soon the others joined in. They hauled some large logs close to the shelter. The women brought armloads of twigs and small branches. Then the fire was lighted and more and more wood was heaped on, until there was a tremendous blaze. "They will see it down in the village," Toko-Batoo said. "They will know that we intend to stay here tonight."

Darkness fell suddenly. The night came down, black and frightening. The little group around the fire sat as close to the flame as they dared, casting many apprehensive glances out into the rim of darkness which shut them in. Already frightened by the night, the lonesome place, and the tiger tracks, they could think of nothing to talk about but witchcraft and magic making. Everyone had a hair-raising story to tell, and Rimau almost joined in with some tales about Gadoh. But something held him back. His memories of Gadoh were so fresh and so painful that he could not spin them into campfire yarns. Perhaps even now Gadoh was pursuing him with his evil magic!

Right in the middle of his thrilling account of how the demons had pulled a woman through the small window of her hut, Toko-Batoo got up and stacked fresh wood on the fire. The whole company scarcely breathed until he sat down again and finished the tale.

When the fresh wood had caught fire, they all stood up, stretched their tired legs and arms, and wrapped themselves in their heavy scarves. Then they climbed up the post supports to the platform of the shelter, which was about six feet above the ground. There they lay down to rest.

"I will lie here on this end of the platform," Toko-Batoo said, as he threw another big log on the flames. "You sleep next to me," he said to Rimau. "I will look after the fire and keep it burning. We need not fear the tiger if the fire is bright."

Rimau muffled himself in his thick scarf and lay down in the spot Toko-Batoo had pointed out. He heard the heavy breathing of his companions. The warmth from the fire was soothing, but he was a little restless, thinking about the tiger.

The village people were tired. They had made the long journey up the mountain and had worked all day digging holes for the coffee plants. The fire cast its warm glow over them. At last they all slept, even Rimau. Toko-Batoo lay at the end of the platform; Rimau was next to him. The logs crackled and snapped in the flames. The fire flared among the shadows, then began to die down. Slowly the big logs became glowing embers and no more flames shot upward. No more brightness flared out into the night. Still everyone slept.

Finally a thick blanket of gray ashes layover the coals that had sparkled earlier in the night. There was little light from the fire any more, and there was no moon. Toko-Batoo stirred. Rimau felt his movement and lazily raised himself on his elbow. Toko-Batoo was climbing down one of the posts that supported the platform. He was going to put more fuel on the fire. Then the boy saw the glitter of fierce eyes in the darkness. He saw the sudden movement of a heavy body and heard Toko-Batoo's cry, as the tigress seized him. The others on the platform, wakened from a sound sleep, screamed in terror and surprise. Toko-Batoo did not let go of the post. He clung to it, screaming, while the huge tigress twisted and growled, dragging at his body. She had fastened her teeth in the man's shoulder and would not let go. For one instant Rimau could not move. Then he sprang off the platform and ran to the fire. He grabbed some dry branches, pushed aside the ashes of the fire, and held the branches against the hot coals underneath. They flared into a torch in

his hand. He leaped toward the tigress and thrust the burning branches into her face. He could smell her whiskers burning. The angry beast gave one more great pull, but Toko-Batoo still held fast to the post. The tigress, with fire in her face and her fur already singed, let go and slunk off into the darkness.

Then the planters piled brush and wood on the fire. It Hamed high into the night, now graying into dawn. Gentle hands drew Toko-Batoo up to the platform. In the light from the fire they could see that his shoulder was deeply wounded. Still, he did not bleed much or seem to suffer much pain. He lay on the platform, moaning softly.

"It is always so," one of the women said, through chattering teeth. "The pain will come later. The wound is numb now."

"Then we must get him back to the village as fast as we can," Rimau said.

Although Rimau had probably saved Toko-Batoo's life, and everyone knew this, the boy felt humiliated and ashamed. He had been sent along to protect the group, and now this terrible thing had happened. He wished he had not slept. Toko-Batoo might die!

The men made a litter from green branches. They wrapped the wounded man in their scarves and laid him on it. The welcome radiance of morning was spreading over the mountains, as they picked up their burden and carried Toko-Batoo carefully and swiftly down the steep path. The company kept close together. They were all in terror of the tigress and feared that she was stalking them even now. They skipped from stone to stone, avoiding slippery places, and hung on to the long *lalang* grass for support.

Before they had reached the village, Toko-Batoo was in great pain. He writhed and groaned on his litter, and when a steep part of the trail caused the men to jerk, he cried out in anguish. Every cry sent a stab through Rimau's heart. If only he had stayed awake! It was all his fault!

77

9.
Jimat and the Tiger

THE LITTLE GROUP WAS JUST APPROACHING THE market green, when those who were in front spied something unusual in the village. A small herd of cattle stood in front of the chief's door.

"Jimat has returned! Jimat has come!" The glad cry went up from every person on the trail—everyone but Rimau. He had never seen his uncle, and he did not want to see him right now. The boy quaked with fear and embarrassment. Surely the chief had already told Jimat how his nephew had come to the village, and how he had entrusted the protection of the coffee planters to his nephew's magic. And now this dreadful thing had happened.

The men who carried the litter walked faster, and soon they stood before the door of Sutan Dolok with their pitiful burden. They called out in loud and mournful tones. People streamed out of the houses, and soon the whole village had gathered together at the chief's door to find out what had happened. Toko-Batoo's wife came too, and when she saw her husband, she began to wail and shriek in a piercing voice.

"Hush!" The chief laid a firm hand on her shoulder. "Jimat is here. He will know what to do." Sutan Dolok motioned to the litter bearers to take the injured man to Jimat's house, which was just three doors away on the same side of the village street.

Then they all saw Jimat. He was coming from the spring, where he had gone to bathe after his long journey. He shouted to them. "What's wrong? Why is there wailing?"

All the men and women who had been at the coffee garden talked at once, trying to tell the witch doctor about the calamity.

Jimat held up his hand and silenced them. "Wait, wait. Let me look first."

Rimau stood beside Toko-Batoo's litter and looked at his uncle. Jimat was a thin man. He stood very straight and looked taller than he really was. He was dark—darker than most of the Battak people. His neck was long and scrawny, and his head was small. But his face was forceful. Rimau examined this face with keen curiosity. Tiny wrinkles fanned out from the corners of Jimat's eyes and mouth. He must smile and laugh a great deal, the boy thought. There were scowl wrinkles between his eyes, too. His face showed that he knew both joy and anger, friendliness and fury, but that a fierce intensity held all these feelings under control. This was no weak man. Rimau looked at him and knew that he was the strongest man in the village—stronger even than Chief Sutan Dolok.

Now Jimat was kneeling beside Toko-Batoo. He uncovered the wounded shoulder, sent for water, and washed it clean. Then, with a wrenching motion, he manipulated the shoulder, and Toko-Batoo screamed until the mountains rang with the echoes.

"It's all right now," Jimat soothed the wounded man. "Your shoulder was pulled out of joint. That's what has been hurting you the most. Now it will feel better. I put it back into place just now." Then Jimat examined the flesh wounds and ordered Toko-Batoo's wife to prepare compresses of crushed leaves. When she brought them he bound them to the shoulder. "Ah, you are a strong man, Toko-Batoo," the medicine man said, with a twinkle in his eye. "That tiger must have given you a mighty jerk to pull your shoulder out of joint like that."

Toko-Batoo didn't say anything but he looked up at Jimat gratefully. The witch doctor told the bearers to carry the injured man to his own house. "I will come over there often during the day," he promised.

Rimau felt comforted. The warm cheerfulness of Jimat's voice made everyone feel better.

They knew now that Toko-Batoo was not as severely injured as they had thought. His shoulder had been dislocated, and that had caused the great pain. The people began to speak in their usual manner and ordinary tones of voice. There was no doubt that Jimat was a great medicine man. Rimau felt too humble to speak to him now, so he turned to go to Toko-Batoo's house with the litter bearers.

Then he felt a hand on his shoulder. It was Jimat's hand; it felt forceful and alive, the way his face looked. No one, Rimau thought, could feel that hand laid on him and ignore it. The boy turned and looked up into his uncle's face.

"You are my sister's son?" The smile wrinkles spread over Jimat's face as he spoke. "The chief has told me about you. He has not told me why you left your father and mother and came here. Would you like to tell me now?"

Rimau told him the whole story of the *chachar* medicine and the anger of the witch doctor, Gadoh. He told of the name feast, of the curse that he had discovered, and of his secret departure in the night. "My mother begged my father to send me to you," he said.

Jimat looked into the boy's eyes and the laughter wrinkles played over his face, like ripples on a wind-blown pool. "She did right!" he said. "I can see why your father sent you away. Where have you been staying?"

Then Rimau told him that he was staying with Toko-Batoo. And he told him about seeing tiger tracks on the northern mountain, and about the tiger trap, and the chief's wish that he go to the coffee garden to protect the planters.

"I think it is best for you to stay on with Toko-Batoo," Jimat said, after a thoughtful pause. "You see, I live alone in my house and I am often away. Sometimes I stay up all night making medicine. You will get better food and better care at Toko-Batoo's house. His wife is a good cook, and she will look after you."

Rimau turned again to leave his uncle, but Jimat called after him, "Let me see your magic mark"

Rimau showed him.

"I have one too," Jimat said, and Rimau saw that the scar on his uncle's arm was newer than his own. "I have persuaded the chief to bring the medicine to this village, also," Jimat said. "I had the medicine scratched on my arm while I was away to buy the cattle. The medicine came to that place, and it was convenient to get it there. The sickness is bad this year."

Jimat visited the wounded man twice that day and changed the poultices on his shoulder. The wound did not hurt as much now. The medicine man told Toko-Batoo, "You are a lucky fellow. You might easily have been killed. As it is, you will only be off your feet for a few days."

"It is all owing to Rimau," Toko-Batoo said. "He saved me from the tiger. He thrust a torch into the tiger's face and that is why I escaped."

Jimat looked at his nephew. "I see why he is called Rimau," he said. "Perhaps he can help us get rid of the tiger."

Tuesday was the weekly market day in Bitter Valley Village. Toko-Batoo, though much better, did not feel well enough to go to market. So he sent Rimau, with several baskets, to bring home coconuts, fruit, and vegetables. Since market was held only once a week, it was necessary to get a good supply.

This market was much smaller than the one beside Lake Toba, where Rimau had gone with his father, but in many ways it was similar. Rimau saw the chief's wife and some of the other women selling cakes of sticky *pooloot*. They stood over big iron kettles of sizzling coconut oil and fried-banana and sweet-potato cakes. The tantalizing fragrance filled the warm air.

Rimau had a few coins left in his moneybag. He took one out and made his way through the group of children who were clamoring for dainties. He bought a handful of cakes and turned away to finish Toko-Batoo's marketing.

At that moment wild screams and shrieks pierced the air. The boy looked around to see what was causing the disturbance. The children around the kettles had scattered like frightened lizards. Rimau's heart leaped to his throat. A man stood beside him, and he heard again the horrible gurgling noise. He saw the hunched shoulders and tangled hair of Kala—the madman. In the bright light of day he looked even more dangerous than by night.

But Kala was not looking at Rimau. He held out both hands for cakes, mumbling in a menacing voice. The chief's wife did not run, but her face was deadly pale. Little Madoo was playing about her feet. She filled the man's hands with cakes. He laughed in a terrifying way and walked toward the trail that led to the mountain where the tiger had seized Toko-Batoo. As Kala walked, the people fell back and left a wide path for him.

Rimau had been too terrified to move from the spot where he was standing when the madman appeared. Now people formed in little groups and began to talk excitedly about Kala. "He is getting bold," one said.

"He has never come to the market before!" A woman hugged her baby to her breast and shivered.

The people watched the figure of Kala grow smaller and smaller, as he went up the path toward the mountain. Then the sound of a gong drew everyone's attention. It had come from the direction of the chief's house. Rimau picked up his full baskets and went to see why the gong had sounded. All the other village people moved in the same direction.

Jimat and Chief Sutan Dolok were standing in front of the chief's house with two strange men. Rimau guessed at once why they had come—the *chachar* medicine. They were going to scratch it on the arms of all the people.

Jimat explained to the village people how fortunate they were to have this wonderful medicine from Padang Lawas. He told how it would protect those who received it from the *chachar* sickness. Then he showed them his own magic mark.

He called Rimau to him and showed the people that Rimau also had the mark.

The chief held out his arm for the scratching, while Jimat lined up the villagers to receive their medicine. Teekoos did not step into theline. He walked up close to the men who were giving the medicine and watched them for a few minutes. Then he walked away, without a word.

The men who brought the medicine were kind. They explained how the fever and soreness would come, how it would soon pass away, and how the magic mark would remain.

When Rimau brought the baskets of food back to the house, Toko-Batoo asked him what was going on. Rimau explained, and Toko-Batoo insisted that the mark be made on his good arm.

In the end, everyone in the village, and many strangers who had come to the market, received the medicine. Jimat's face glowed with satisfaction. Teekoos alone failed to get the medicine. He had disappeared and could not be found.

Then the people went back to the market place. Here and there they sat in groups on the grass and talked about the *chachar* medicine and about Kala and about the tiger which had hurt Toko-Batoo's shoulder. The green buzzed with excited voices. Rimau came out of Toko-Batoo's house and went from one group to another, listening to the stories the people were telling about tigers and madmen. Then he felt a hand on his shoulder. He knew the touch of that hand. It was Jimat's.

"My son," the medicine man began, "there is important business for us to attend to on the mountain." He motioned to Rimau to follow him and set out toward the mountain where the planters had spent the night.

The boy fastened up his sarong and pulled his green velvet cap down tight on his head. His heart was beating fast. What business could they have on that mountain together, he wondered. The tiger? It must be the tiger!

"The magic of the tigers is in your blood," Jimat said, as they left the crowded market place and started up the long slope of the mountain.

The Tiger of Bitter Valley

Two or three hours ago Kala had followed this same path. The madman must be somewhere about on the mountain. Rimau began to feel apprehensive. Was Jimat going to take him out on the mountain and leave him there to work his tiger magic?

"We must do something about this tigress," the older man said. "None of the people will work in the gardens until we get rid of her. How well did you see her?"

"When I was in the tree, as you know, I watched a tigress and her young one for several hours," Rimau told his uncle. "I think it was the same tigress which attacked Toko-Batoo, though I could not see her very well that night. The tracks looked the same, but I couldn't find the cub's footprints."

"Well, we will learn more about it tonight." Jimat scratched his nose with the fringe of his scarf.

Rimau was frightened. So they were going back to the coffee garden to spend the night with the tigress! He looked at Jimat. The witch doctor carried a belt knife, like all the other Battak men. Rimau had one too; otherwise, they were unarmed. A short belt knife was a poor weapon to depend on when there was a full-grown tigress at large. Still, he felt his courage coming back. Jimat was cheerful and confident; he must have strong magic against tigers.

"Do you think Kala lives on this mountain?" the boy asked.
"Have you seen Kala?" His uncle was surprised.

"He came to the market just now-just before the gong was beaten. He took many cakes from the women and he came up this way."

Jimat stopped in the path and looked all around. He motioned for Rimau to be quiet and listened for several minutes. Then he led the way again along the mountain slope. "We think Kala lives on this mountain," Jimat said, "but we don't know where. Maybe he stays in several different places. I do not think we need be afraid of him today. He is full of cakes." Then Jimat sighed and looked sadder than the boy had ever seen him. "Oh, you should have known Kala when"—he stopped—"before he got like this. He was one to take the heart!"

Finally they stopped to rest, for the climb was getting steeper. "I brought you along because the village people have confidence in your magic," Jimat said. "They believe that you drove the tigers from the northern mountain. Also you saved Toko-Batoo from a tiger on this mountain." Jimat leaned against a rock and rested.

"But I didn't drive the tigers from the northern mountain. They went of their own accord," Rimau said. "And if I had stayed awake, Toko-Batoo might not have been attacked."

"All the same, no boy who thrusts a burning torch in the face of a tiger can be a coward," Jimat said. "I think you should learn to be a medicine man."

"But my father is a Mamora chief," the boy reminded him.

"I don't forget that." Jimat smiled. "You will be chief someday too. But learning good magic will help you, whatever you are. It will make you a good chief." He added in a lower voice, "While I was in Padang Lawas, I learned about some new medicine that is more powerful than anythan we have ever had in our villages. I will teach you about it."

"Then I will learn," the boy said.

They began to climb again and were silent for some distance. They passed under the great rock of Nangir-Jati and came to the top of a steep part of the path. Rimau was wondering about the new medicine. He had forgotten, for the moment, the dangers of the mountain.

Then suddenly, without any warning, they saw the tigress! She was crouched in the path directly in front of them! Her nose was lifted and her nostrils twitched. The bands of black and orange on her body glistened in the sunshine. The man and the boy froze where they were, while the tigress glared at them. She bared her teeth in a snarl, and her thick tail lashed from side to side.

Then the mountain rang with her frightful roar! Rimau jumped, his heart in his throat. Jimat tore the scarf from his shoulder and ran at the tigress, shrieking and waving it. Still the great beast did not move. She crouched in the path, her tail moving slowly from side to side. Her green eyes were nar-

rowed and glowed with a wicked-looking light; her muscles were tensed, ready to spring. Jimat was almost upon her. Then Rimau screamed and also ran toward the tigress, waving his scarf. The great cat bounded lightly to her feet, retreated a few steps, and slithered into the grass without a sound.

"We must go back!" Jimat whispered to Rimau. "We have seen our enemy, and she is heading toward the village!" The two ran back down the mountain path, leaping from rock to rock. Rimau stayed close to Jimat in their headlong flight. He glanced back once in a while to see if the tigress was following them, but neither of them paused until they reached the market green in front of the village.

Market was over. The people had gone. As they walked to the chief's door, Rimau told Jimat he was sure now that the tigress they had just seen was the one he had watched from the tree on the northern mountain.

"Come out! Come out!" Jimat called at the chief's door. Sutan Dolok stuck out his turbaned head.

"We met the tiger near Nangir-Jati," the witch doctor said. "It is the tigress Rimau saw on the northern mountain. She is young and strong and well-grown. She is coming this way. We frightened her, but she will come—she will come to this village!"

Several people had come out of their houses. They knew that Jimat had taken Rimau to the mountain. There was great distress when they heard that the tigress was still on the near slope of the mountain. Mothers gathered their children into their arms. The men began rounding up goats, ponies, and water buffaloes. A silent misery settled over the villagers. This tigress had taken many of their animals. She had severely wounded Toko-Batoo. Now she was coming down to the village!

10.
Teekoos

THAT NIGHT IT BEGAN TO RAIN—A HEAVY, DRENCH-ing rain that swelled the little river and kept the villagers busy protecting their rice fields. They toiled in the pouring rain, opening and closing the bamboo drains in the mud walls that divided one section of a rice field from another. This had to be done to keep the growing rice from being flooded and drowned by the deluge of water, and also to prevent the mud walls from being washed out between the fields.

Toko-Batoo had worked hard on his large field of rice, but now he was unable to leave his mat because of his wound. So when the heavy rains began, Rimau went to work in the field with Toko-Batoo's wife. He waded waist-high in the soft mud of the rice fields. He strengthened the mud walls and straightened any plants that were bent. He learned to regulate the flow of water in different sections of the field. After a couple of days, he took over all the responsibility for the rice field and worked alone there. This left Toko-Batoo's wife free to care for her husband and cook the meals. For several days the boy came home at sundown feeling very tired. He saw little of his uncle, for Jimat had his own rice field to look after. The field next to Toko-Batoo's was owned by Teekoos. During the days Rimau worked in the rain he saw a great deal of the Rat. Everyone in the village had become sick from the *chachar* medicine; by the end of a week, only Jimat, Rimau, and Teekoos were able to work in the fields. Then their responsibilities increased, for Jimat insisted that the sick folk stay indoors. He assigned extra duties to Rimau and Teekoos, and the three of them tried to handle the most pressing work in all the rice fields.

A tiny shelter had been built between the fields where Teekoos and Rimau worked. They often went to this place to eat their noonday meal of cold rice, because it was protected from the pelting rain. "What do you think about this magic mark that is making everyone sick?" Teekoos asked one day while they ate.

Rimau glanced down at his own scar, and said, "I have heard that the *chachar* sickness has no power against those who have the magic mark"

Teekoos snorted with anger. "It is foreign witchcraft!" he declared. "It will make the spirits angry, and trouble will come! You wait and see! Trouble will come!" The Rat spluttered and spit in his excitement. His small eyes took on a wicked gleam. "It is the chief who called the foreign magic here. It is the chief who will get into trouble! You wait and see!"

Rimau never felt at ease with Teekoos, and now there was such malice in his face and such pent-up fury in his whole attitude that the boy felt fear rising in his stomach. He hurriedly finished his rice and went back to work. That night the tigress killed a water buffalo right at the edge of the village green where the market was held. The following morning the sun shone for the first time in many days. Jimat and the chief saw the buffalo's carcass from the village and walked out to examine it. The chief still had a sore red arm, but Paksa's arm was getting well fast and he and Rimau went along to see the dead buffalo. It was half-eaten.

"It is certainly the doing of that tigress," Jimat said. "She will probably come back tonight to finish her feast. I wish we had a fire stick. We could certainly kill that tiger with a fire stick."

"Why don't you go to the market place in Sipirok and ask the officer there to lend us his fire stick?" the chief said. "Tell him about our trouble, and I'm sure he will let you have it. He knows that you understand how to work those fire sticks. You will not return in time to shoot the tigress tonight, but we will be able to hunt her later."

"I'll go right now," Jimat said. Then he laid his hand on Rimau's arm and led him along toward the village. "I'm trusting you to see that things go well here till tomorrow, when I come back. The village people have faith in you, and so do I."

Rimau was about to object. He knew that the village might be troubled by the tigress at any moment, but he looked into Jimat's face and saw that his uncle really believed in him. He said quietly, "I will do the best I can."

Late that afternoon, after Rimau had finished working in the rice fields, he was playing a game with Paksa. They kneeled, tossing small stones into the air, catching them, and keeping score.

Little Madoo stood behind the boys as they played. "Madoo wants pretty flowers!" she said several times. But the boys were so interested in their game that they paid no attention to her. She was talking about a vine that grew on the house by the river where Kala used to live. It bore small pink flowers, which grew in bright, tempting sprays.

When the sun went down, the chief's wife came out of the house and looked around for the little girl. "Isn't Madoo here with you?" she asked, fright creeping into her voice.

Rimau jumped to his feet. "She was here. I think I heard her a minute ago—but it could have been longer than that. She wanted flowers." Then Rimau remembered the vine on Kala's house. Madoo must have seen it and wanted to pick the beautiful flowers. As he ran toward the house that stood all alone on the other side of the river, his heart beat fast. Beads of sweat stood out on his forehead. The house was close to the place where he had struggled with Kala, and he suspected that the madman often returned to lurk about his old home.

It was already quite dark outside, but Paksa came running behind him. They found the tiny girl beside Kala's house. Her hands were full of the pink blossoms and she was laughing and talking. "Hurry back and tell your mother she is safe," Rimau said to Paksa. "I will carry her."

Paksa darted away toward his father's house. Rimau lifted the child and, turning his back resolutely on the forbidding darkness of the house, he walked toward the chief's door.

Then he saw Teekoos crossing the bridge that led into the village. The Rat stopped when he reached Rimau and looked at him. He saw the flowers and knew where Rimau had been. He saw Madoo. His face darkened with anger. "How dared you take the chief's daughter to the house of the evil spirits?" he stormed. "Give her to me!"

He tried to take the little girl from Rimau's arms, but Madoo screamed and clung to the boy. Teekoos drew back and in a burst of fury slapped the child smartly on her fat cheek.

The anger Rimau felt then was so great that he considered fighting Teekoos on the spot, but he had Madoo in his arms. She was sobbing. Teekoos walked away and entered the chief's house. A moment later Madoo's mother came hurrying down the path and gathered the weeping child into her arms.

Rimau went home, sat down on the mat beside Toko-Batoo, and told him what had happened. "Teekoos seems to wish the chief evil," the boy said. "Why is that?"

"There are many reasons," Toko-Batoo said, after a thoughtful pause. "He expected to be appointed chief counselor, but Sutan Dolok chose Kala instead. He has never forgiven the chief for that."

"Who is chief counselor now?" the boy asked.

"Didn't the chief appoint someone else after Kala became mad?"

"I am chief counselor now," Toko-Batoo said with pride.

Rimau thought about this for a minute. "Then the chief didn't appoint Teekoos even after Kala could no longer be chief counselor."

91

"That is right," Toko-Batoo said. "The chief thinks it possible that Teekoos made an evil charm against Kala. The chief doesn't trust him, and Teekoos knows it."

"Wasn't Teekoos on the mountain with Kala the time he got the madness?" Rimau asked.

"Yes. He was the last one to see the true Kala. They went to plant coffee, and Teekoos came back that same day. He said Kala wanted to stay longer. But the chief thinks they may have had a quarrel and that Teekoos made an evil charm."

"That's a strange thing, isn't it?" Rimau said, as much to himself as to Toko-Batoo. "Teekoos returned alone. Yet a Battak man never goes anywhere without a friend, if he has one, and friends do not usually part on long journeys."

"Yes, it is queer," Toko-Batoo agreed. "Teekoos is a charm maker, you know, and since the trouble with Kala, his charms have not been wanted much. He blames the chief for that, too."

"And he is very angry about the *chachar* medicine," Rimau remembered. "He became furious when he talked to me about it the other day in the rice field."

Darkness had fallen while they talked, and soon it was night. Toko-Batoo slept now, and the house was quiet. Rimau heard a call in front of the door. He opened it and was surprised to see Paksa standing outside.

"Come with me," he said to Rimau in a low voice. "Let us go and climb the mango tree close to the place where the tigress killed the buffalo. Maybe we will see her come back tonight. We can watch and see which direction she comes from." Rimau was thrilled with this plan. It would be fun to hide in the mango tree with his friend. He wrapped his scarf about his shoulders.

The two boys hurried to the mango tree, making as little noise as possible. With silent, catlike movements they swung themselves up among the thick branches, taking care to sit where they would have a clear view of the buffalo's carcass. They whispered to one another as they crouched there. They knew they must be quiet, for the tiger might come at any time.

They had climbed the tree early in the night, and they waited for over two hours. The moon shone on the dead buffalo, for the carcass was not close enough to the tree to be hidden by its shadow. They watched now with every sense keyed to the movement of a twig or the rustle of a leaf.

Then it came! Not the tiger they had expected, but a thin, crouching figure, which crept toward the tiger's kill. The boys almost gasped aloud. This was a man—a human being! He threw himself on the carcass of the buffalo and, with gulping noises, began to feed ravenously on the raw flesh.

Rimau knew who it was. The memory of his struggle with this terrible creature was still fresh. Paksa was in a panic of fright; he almost fell from the tree. Rimau put one arm around him to steady him. Together the two watched—breathless, shocked.

Only a few minutes after the man had come, a soft padding sound in the brush alerted the two watchers in the mango tree. The tigress broke through the bushes on the side toward the southern mountain. She walked boldly toward her kill and the human creature slunk off into the brush without a sound. The tigress appeared to take no notice of this intrusion and fell to her feast of buffalo meat.

For an hour she gorged herself, then padded off in the direction from which she had come. After she had disappeared the boys waited several minutes. Then they came down from their lookout post. "Does your father know you came out here?" Rimau asked, suddenly realizing what they had done, and afraid of what the chief might say.

"No, he doesn't know," Paksa said. "I crawled out my window, and I left it open a little, so I can crawl in again."

"I don't think you should do that," Rimau said. "We might have gotten into a great deal of trouble tonight. I didn't tell Toko-Batoo where I was going, either. Now I will have to wake him up, so he can let me into the house."

"Do you think I should tell my father now?" Paksa asked.

"That is the right thing for you to do," Rimau said. "And I

will tell Toko-Batoo."

When Toko-Batoo heard the story of how the two boys had watched the madman and the tiger from their perch in the tree, he was pale with fright and anger. "I know your magic is strong, Tiger Boy," he said, "but you must never go out in the night like that again."

When Rimau awoke the next morning, the sun was shining and the birds singing. The terror of last night seemed far away, like a dream. But when Jimat arrived early in the afternoon with the fire stick, the boy told his uncle all that had happened during his absence.

Jimat looked at Rimau with reproach. "I am not afraid for you," he said, "but beware where you take Paksa. If anything happens to that boy, the chief will die! You know about Kala, and the chief lost his two older sons from sickness—*chachar* sickness."

"But it was Paksa who thought of watching from the tree," Rimau said. "Really?" Jimat looked surprised. "I wouldn't have expected that. He must be braver than I thought."

Now Rimau understood why Paksa had not been allowed to go along to inspect the tiger trap or to the mountain garden to plant coffee. Yet he knew that Paksa was as quick and strong as himself.

When Rimau learned that his uncle intended to hunt the tiger the next day, he asked if Paksa and he might go along. Jimat consented but smiled at the idea of Paksa's coming. He was very surprised when Sutan Dolok gave his permission. Paksa was glad, and he and Rimau were filled with a shivery delight at the prospect of the tiger hunt.

11.
Tiger Hunt

JIMAT CHOSE THE MEN HE WANTED TO TAKE ON the tiger hunt. "The chief must go," he said. "And Teekoos must go, because he is the best spear thrower. The two boys will go, and we must have three other men to help build the blind. They can return home before dark."

It was decided that they would take a goat along as bait for the tiger, and they planned to start about midmorning of the next day. Jimat was anxious to kill the tigress before more of their animals were attacked. The chief was especially proud of the cattle just brought from Padang Lawas, and he had no intention of sharing them with the tigress. Excitement spread through the village like a fire. The people talked of nothing else but the tiger hunt.

Late that afternoon Rimau and Paksa were walking on the bank beside the little river. They often did this toward the end of the day, for they could have a quiet talk as they strolled along the river. Today they decided not to go far because of the tiger.

Along the riverbank the ground was open, except for the short grass. The running water, which had cut a deep channel, made a pleasant sound as it cascaded over the rocks in its course. Neither of the boys had spoken for some time. Their bare feet made no sound on the grass. Because of this and the music of the river, Teekoos did not hear them as they approached. When the boys looked down from the bank—here about twelve feet above the river-they saw Teekoos, crouched on a narrow strip of sand at the water's edge. Rimau and Paksa stopped and stood perfectly still. Neither of them could guess what the Rat was doing. His belt knife lay on the sand, and he was stirring something in half of a coconut shell. He was intent on what he was doing and kept his back toward the boys.

First he polished the knife in the sand and wiped it clean on his scarf. Then, very carefully, he dipped his finger into the mixture he had been stirring and smeared a thick layer of it all over one side of the knife blade. Then he swung the knife through the air again and again, mumbling to himself all the time. He put down the knife, with the smeared side of the blade lying upward in the evening sunlight, and leaned forward to wash his hands in the stream. The boys were still staring, overcome by curiosity. Now Teekoos lifted the knife again and drew it swiftly through the air. Again he laid it on the sand.

Rimau looked at Paksa and signaled to him to come away. Protected by the noise of the stream, they withdrew without being observed. They did not speak until they were back on the village green. "What do you suppose he was doing?" Paksa asked.

"I haven't any idea," Rimau said. "He smeared something on the knife, and it sounded to me as if he was mumbling some sort of spell over it." He took off his green cap and scratched his head. "Maybe the knife was getting rusty. You know how Teekoos loves his knives."

Paksa was not convinced. "But why did he have to go down by the river and hide while he was doing it?" he questioned.

"Well, I don't like the look of it either, but I don't like anything Teekoos does. He—wait! I know what he was doing. He was getting ready for the tiger hunt!"

"No one prepares a belt knife for a tiger. We use spears!" Paksa retorted.

97

The Tiger of Bitter Valley

They had come now to the door of the chief's house. Here they stood in silence for a moment. Neither of them could forget what they had just seen, and yet neither of them could explain it.

"Aren't you glad you are going on the tiger hunt?" Rimau said, his face brightening. "You and I will probably find out what it's all about tomorrow." At this, a smile spread over Paksa's round face, and Rimau left him at his door and turned to walk toward Toko-Batoo's house. He saw Teekoos, just now returning. A smug smile played around his small, round mouth. He did not speak to Rimau but hurried to his own hut.

The next day, in the middle of the forenoon, the hunters started out. They had a long climb up the mountain ahead of them, and they planned to find a good spot to await the tigress and complete all arrangements well before sundown. The chief's wife and Toko-Batoo's wife had prepared *pooloot* cakes and curried chicken, which the men carried in banana-leaf packages. Teekoos brought along two good-sized papayas—delicious melons with juicy orange-colored flesh.

"I wish Teekoos had stayed at home," Paksa whispered to Rimau, as they walked behind the others on the rocky trail toward the mountain gardens. They were just passing the spot where the water buffalo had been killed.

"There isn't anything we can do about it," Rimau replied. "Jimat is glad to have him along. Isn't he the best spear thrower in the village?"

Jimat led the goat they planned to use as bait slowly over the rocks. Sometimes, when the way was difficult, he picked up the little animal and carried it. "They will tether the goat on the mountainside, and when he cries in the night, the tiger will come for him," Rimau said to Paksa.

As the hunters climbed they looked constantly from side to side, examining the trees and shrubs and the lay of the land. They were looking for a suitable place to hide and await the tigress—one not too far away from her lair or from the spot where she had made her last kill. Among the loose rocks at the base of

N angir-J ati the hunters discovered a place to their liking. It was Jimat's opinion that the tigress had made her den somewhere on the huge rock. Rimau remembered the day at the mountain garden when he had seen something moving on the sharp ridge at the top of the rock. Could it have been the tigress?

The hunters had selected for their blind a sharp upthrust of rock screened by a branching tree. Here they could sit on the rock in comparative safety, while they watched their enemy approach the goat. The small creature was tied in a dusty basin of bare ground, about twenty paces from the rock where they planned to conceal themselves.

When the arrangements had been made, and the goat tied in place, it was already late afternoon. They were all tired, and even though they knew there was a spring a little farther up the path, they decided to eat their lunch where they were and look for water later.

When Teekoos brought out his papayas, everyone exclaimed with joy. These would quench their thirst. Teekoos handed the melons to Jimat, who looked around and counted the eight persons who must share the two melons. He cut each one in half and was about to divide the halves into fourths, when Teekoos reached over and took back one of the melon halves.

"We will share," he said to the chief, who sat beside him. He drew out his belt knife and raised it to divide the piece of melon.

Then something awoke in Rimau's brain. Teekoos hated the chief. Why was he so friendly with him? Why was he sitting by him? This was the knife Teekoos had polished yesterday beside the stream! Which side was the smeared side? What was it smeared with? These questions ran confusedly through Rimau's mind, as he moved closer and watched the Rat. Teekoos drew his knife and made a clean cut through the melon, handing the piece on the right to the chief. This was according to polite custom. The look on the Rat's face was secret and ugly. Rimau remembered stories of knives which had been poisoned. Swiftly the boy's mind worked as he considered what to do. In another instant Sutan Dolok would pick up the

piece of melon and bite into it. The boy, who now had moved very close to the chief, made a quick movement. As he shifted his position he flicked the fringe of his scarf in the dust, where they sat. Then he shook his scarf, so that the dust fell on the papaya in the chief's hand.

Sutan Dolok's face darkened with annoyance.

"Oh, I'm so sorry! Excuse me, please!" Rimau exclaimed. "Let me take it!" He picked up his own piece of melon and handed it to the chief. Then he took his belt knife and carefully trimmed away all the exposed surface of the piece of papaya he had spoiled. As he bit into the melon, he looked Teekoos full in the face. The fury in his small eyes shocked Rimau. He felt sure now that Teekoos had used a poisoned knife to cut the chief's piece of melon. Did Teekoos know that he had shaken dust on the melon on purpose? It was unlikely that he did, but nevertheless he would hate Rimau for frustrating his plan. Rimau knew that he had planned to put an end to the chief's life because of his unending hatred of him and his jealousy of Kala. Had he tried to kill Kala, too, and failed? Well, his plan had failed today. Rimau had spoiled it, and the boy realized that Teekoos would now seek revenge on him as well as on the chief.

The boy looked around at the rest of the company, seated in a circle. They had no knowledge of what had taken place. Even Paksa did not understand. Everyone was eating rice and curried chicken with good appetite, and Jimat was happy and excited. Rimau saw that the witch doctor was hopeful that now the village would be rid of the tigress. He laughed and talked with the chief. The other men joked and chatted with one another. Only Teekoos was sullen, and Rimau noticed that the Rat's narrowed eyes were often on him.

"Now our three helpers may go home," Jimat said. "And you two boys may return with them, if you like."

Rimau knew that the fewer the hunters, the better chance they had of catching the tigress. Still he was unwilling to leave. He looked at Paksa, knowing that he felt the same way. "We

101

would like to stay," Rimau said, speaking for both of them. But he could not speak of his main reason for wanting to stay: Teekoos' secret urge for revenge. He had been foiled once; perhaps he could be outwitted or exposed another time. Rimau was overwhelmed by what had just taken place. He felt like someone in a dream. What if he and Paksa had not taken that walk last night? What if they had not seen the Rat smearing his knife?

The three men who had come along to help build the blind hurried away down the mountain in the late sunlight. Those who were left began to plan how best to arrange themselves. As night came on, the five hunters concealed themselves in the blind. Jimat prepared the fire stick, and Teekoos and the chief examined their spears. "Do nothing until the tiger reaches the goat. Then I shall shoot," Jimat told them. "If I miss, and the tiger comes this way, throw your spears."

It was getting dark now and they waited in silence. No one moved or whispered. The goat, perhaps aware of the danger, began to bleat pitifully. It strained on its tether and circled the basin where it was tied. Every few minutes it raised its head and bleated. The hunters knew that if the tigress was within hearing distance, she would surely come.

The moon rose behind Nangir-Jati and spread a glow over the mountainside. Far up—hundreds of feet above them—there was a slight noise. It sounded as if a stone was bouncing down the slope. It might be the tigress. Everyone peered into the moonlit night and waited, on edge. Jimat squatted; his fire stick pointed toward the goat. It lay across the sharp rock in front of him, ready to fire.

There was another slight sound of falling gravel—nearer now. It must be the tigress. The waiting had become almost painful, as the watchers on the rock strained to hear the smallest movement in the darkness.

Then, from the very foot of the rock where they waited, a huge form crept toward the tethered goat. Slowly the great beast inched herself along the ground. Jimat aimed his fire stick at the goat. The tigress was creeping toward the frightened animal with stealthy grace.

She was halfway across the open spot of ground.

Then Teekoos uttered a fierce cry, and his spear flew through the air. With a roar, the tigress leaped into the air and made off through the rocks.

"This man is the king of fools!" Jimat said in hot anger. "Now all our trouble is for nothing!" He took Teekoos by the shoulder and shook him. "Didn't you hear me say I would fire when the tigress leaped for the goat, and only if I missed, were you to throw your spear?"

Teekoos didn't answer.

"Wait—wait!" the chief interrupted. "Maybe Teekoos wounded her. I think he did. She may be very angry and may be waiting to spring on us from those rocks if we leave now! We must stay right here until daylight."

All the rest of the night Jimat complained about what Teekoos had done, and the Rat sat silent and morose. When morning finally lighted the mountain, Teekoos seemed to revive. "I know I wounded her," he said. "When the sun is high enough we shall follow her and kill her."

"No. We will not go with you," Jimat said, still angry. "You only frightened her away. I'm sure you will not find one drop of blood on the ground."

And it was so. In the morning light they investigated the place thoroughly. They could see the huge tracks, but no blood could be found to show that the animal had been wounded. The spear, however, was gone.

"You see! My spear is gone!" Teekoos whined. "It must have struck the tiger."

"Perhaps it did," Jimat said scornfully, as he looked all around for the spear. "Maybe the tiger has carried your spear away. But what is the use of being a good spear thrower if you can't obey orders?"

Even before they entered the village, everyone knew they had not killed the tiger. It is the custom of tiger hunters to skin the beast on the spot, stuff the hide with grass, and carry it home on a pole in triumph. There was no hide—no pole—no triumph. Jimat told everyone what had happened. "The tigress will certainly come to the village again!" he warned them.

Teekoos slunk away to his hut. The people gathered in the village green to ask questions of the other hunters and to bemoan their bad luck. They knew that more water buffaloes would be killed, more goats, more ponies—and perhaps even people.

12.
Nangir-Jati

RIMAU LEFT THE VILLAGE GREEN AND WENT TO Jimat's house. "My uncle," he began, "I think it is Teekoos' intention to harm the chief."

"What makes you think that?" Jimat asked in surprise.

"Did you see him divide the papaya melon with the chief yesterday? I am sure his knife was poisoned on one side."

"How do you know?" Jimat took the boy by the shoulders and looked sternly into his eyes. "This is a terrible thing you are saying."

Then Rimau told how he and Paksa had seen Teekoos on the riverbank, preparing the knife.

"So that is why you threw dust on the chief's piece of melon and gave him yours!" Jimat loosened his hold on the boy's shoulders and took a step backward, regarding him with something like admiration in his eyes.

"There was no other way," the boy said.

Jimat scowled and twisted his scarf. He appeared to be in deep thought. At last he spoke. "Don't tell anyone of this," he said. "There is no way to prove it. I think you are right in your suspicions. He wants to injure Sutan Dolok, because he brought the *chachar* medicine here."

"There are greater reasons than that," Rimau said.

"Yes, yes. There could be other very important reasons. He will try again. We must find some way to stop him."

After breakfast the next morning Rimau and Paksa were sitting on the sand at the river's edge. They had made a small net and were casting it in one of the rocky pools, hoping to catch some small fish. They were near Kala's house by the river, but they could not see it because the riverbank behind them was very high.

They could hear bees humming around the vine of flowers that grew on the deserted house. Rimau thought of Paksa's sister. "We should have brought Madoo," he said. "She would have fun here."

"She would make noise, too," Paksa objected. "We can't catch fish if there's noise."

Then both boys heard a sound; it was Madoo's voice. She must have followed them. Perhaps she was pulling flowers from the vine on the old house. The boys left their net and sprang up the bank, just as a frightened scream rang out from behind the house. They burst through the weeds that surrounded the house and ran around to the back, but Madoo was not there. They stopped and looked at one another.

"I'm sure that was Madoo's voice," Paksa said.

Then they heard the sound of running feet. Flying along the path to the southern mountain, was a gaunt, ragged figure. They heard another faint scream. Madoo was being carried off by the madman Kala!

Horrified, the two boys screamed with all their might. But Kala only hurried faster. Rimau glimpsed Madoo's mother, standing in the doorway of the chief's house. Faintly he heard her piercing shriek, when she saw what had happened. Then he heard nothing but the pounding of blood in his temples, as he and Paksa gave chase.

The two boys were no match for the wild creature who had lived in the open for two years. Like a jungle animal, he leaped from rock to rock up the mountain trail. He had used his ragged scarf to tie the baby to his back. The boys caught glimpses of him up the slope and knew that he was far ahead of them and gaining distance.

They gasped for breath, but still they ran on and on. Jimat and the chief and most of the other men in the village were working in the rice fields in the other direction. It would be an hour or two before the women could find them and tell them what had happened. Only Teekoos was in the village. Rimau had seen him just before he went to the river to fish.

The boys stumbled and groaned, as they ran up the steep slope. Once again they caught sight of the fleeing figure high above them. Then they saw him no more. Discouraged and exhausted, they sank down in the path. But, sick with terror at the thing that had happened, they got up again and went on as fast as they could run. They had made the mistake of running too fast at first and now, as the ascent became steeper, they were completely winded.

"We do wrong to be so terrified," Rimau gasped, as he laid his hand on Paksa's arm. They had paused for a moment out of necessity. Breathing had become an agony. "It is not good for us to be afraid."

Paksa could not answer for a little while. He lay on the ground, his chest heaving. "I heard Jimat telling my father that the Great Good Spirit comes to help those who need," he said.

"Did Jimat say such a thing? That is odd. Our witch doctors in Toba know only the evil spirits." Rimau had caught his breath now.

"The village men will follow us as soon as my mother tells them," Paksa said. "I know she saw us. But it will take a long time to call the men from the rice fields."

"It will take too long." Rimau stood up. "We must overtake Kala and bring Madoo home."

They started up the path again, going a little slower now. "Kala is stronger than any man I have ever known," Rimau said. "We shall not take the child from him easily. Besides, he may have already—"

"No, no!" Paksa interrupted him. "We must not think of that. We will do the best we can. I'm sure the Good Spirit will help us."

They had come to the foot of Nangir-Jati. The sound of a falling stone made them both look up. Hundreds of feet above on the treacherous rocks, something must be moving. They looked at one another. They were now so close to the great rock that they could not see up its steep precipice. Could Kala be ascending the rock? It must be so! Kala, the madman, was climbing these dizzy steeps where no other man had dared to go, or even thought it possible to go. He was carrying Madoo. Would that added burden cause him to stumble and fall?

"How can we go up?" they asked each other. "How can we climb Nangir-Jati?" Yet they knew there was no other way. They examined the base of the cliff, seeking some way to climb it. If Kala had gone up the rock, there must be a way to follow. It was half an hour before they found a break in the jungle that grew densely around the rock's base. They could see that this pathway had been used. They advanced slowly up the path, for in many places they had to pull themselves up, using bushes and vines and the roots of trees. When they paused at intervals to catch their breath, the silence of the place frightened them. It was damp and darkly shadowed by creepers and overhanging trees. Wet branches scratched their faces. After a while the path was no longer distinct, and they were not sure Kala had gone this way. They only knew that he must be high on the rock of Nangir-Jati and that they must scale it at any cost.

Now, as they struggled for footholds, the rock seemed a living, malignant thing. Thick, wet moss filled its chinks and cracks. Once Rimau slipped to his waist in a crevasse filled with it. Out of the moss grew trees, some of them very large. Yet they were as unstable as growing rice. When the boys leaned against them they wavered and swayed, as though planted in water. Rimau had a terrifying feeling that the whole mass of moss and trees might loosen and drop off, carrying them with it down to the valley below. How could they climb such a rock? How could they hope to reach the summit? Perhaps Kala had already fallen from some high pinnacle, and now he and Madoo might be lying at the foot of Nangir-Jati!

They found a spring of water gushing from the face of the rock. They drank, and Rimau said, "Let us not be discouraged. There must be a Good Spirit. If Jimat says there is, I believe it. The Good Spirit will make our feet like the feet of the mountain deer or the claws of the tiger. We will reach the top of Nangir-Jati."

They began climbing again. They were now several hundred feet up the steep rock. It seemed to Rimau that his ears buzzed and whistled with strange and eerie sounds. His head was aching and felt as if it would burst from the mighty effort of climbing. His hands were bleeding from the sharp edges of the rock and the rough branches, but he paid no attention to that. On and on, up and up, the two climbed. Now the moss grew shorter. There was no longer any moisture for trees, nothing but rock covered with short gray moss. How could they go on?

Finally the two lifted their heads over the last ledge of rock and gazed out over a steep ridge, which slanted upward. This rocky ridge fell away on both sides to depths that could only be imagined. The top of it looked as sharp as a knife blade. One side of the ridge was the precipice of Nangir-Jati that could be seen from the village. Now they could see that the other side of the ridge was a precipice, just as steep, that faced away from the village. These precipices were so smooth, and slanted down so sharply on both sides, that one could not hope to venture onto them without slipping off. Yet there was no other way to go.

Rimau put out his hand and felt the surface of the rock. The moss that covered it was slippery, as if it were wet, but it was thicker and deeper than he had thought. Had Kala crossed this dreadful place without slipping? It seemed unlikely. How could any creature climb along this sharp ridge? Then from far up, near the jagged peak of Nangir-Jati, they heard a faint cry. It must be Madoo! There was only one way to reach her. They must cross this knifelike ridge of rock—but how?

"Come. I know how we can do it," Rimau said. "We can hang by our hands from the top edge of the ridge and go across hand over hand." He grasped the top of the sharp ridge, but he quickly let himself down beside Paksa again.

"The rock is too sharp. My hands would not take me across. We can't do that!"

Both boys studied the ridge again, and then Rimau had another idea. "Let us take each other by the hand. You walk on one side of the ridge, and I shall walk on the other. We shall hold each other tightly, bracing ourselves, and set our feet firmly in the moss. We shall not look at the precipices; we shall look straight ahead, for that is where we shall find Madoo!"

There was no other way. They joined hands and stood on either side of the ridge, leaning far out at an angle to the rock. It worked! They did not look down and did not see the sheer precipices extending downward—or how far below they ended. They held one another with an iron grasp and turned their eyes forward and up—up to the heights of the rock. They took a few steps; then, having found their balance, they went faster. High on the ridge of Nangir-Jati, they raced like mountain goats. Shouts and cries from the valley below ascended in the warm noonday air. Even then they did not look down or slacken their mad rush across and up the knifelike ridge of the great rock.

For two hundred feet they balanced themselves, crossing to the upper end of the ridge. There they found a firm foothold and rested a little. They saw a faint path among the rocks and followed it. Could it be that Kala had made this terrible place his lair for two years? Could it be that he had crossed, and recrossed, the steep, jagged ridge many times and still remained alive? It seemed impossible; yet it was probably so.

Now all their thoughts were of Madoo. Was she still alive? Rimau felt a sudden sickness. There was no sign of Kala or the child, no sound—nothing to show them that any other person was on the pinnacle ahead. Where could the child be? At every turn of the path they became more anxious.

Then they came to the cave. Its opening was among the rocks just ahead of them. A little way inside the entrance lay Madoo on a ragged scarf. She seemed to be asleep. Kala was nowhere in sight, and Rimau guessed that he was sleeping in the cave. He picked up the baby and bound her firmly to his back with his scarf, knotting the scarf ends across his chest. She still slept. He felt her limp body against his back. It was warm and soft, and Rimau felt wonder and gratitude.

Now the boys thought of Kala again. He might come out of the cave at any moment. They had moved softly and whispered, but who could tell how sharp Kala's ears might be? He would be angry when he found that Madoo was gone, and he would surely follow them. There was no time to lose! They hurried down the rocky path and paused for only a moment when they came to the upper end of the ridge. Again they joined hands. The burden on Rimau's back made him the heavier of the two, so they had to find a new balance. They hung precariously, their hands clasped. Then slowly they started across the dreadful two hundred feet that lay between them and the lesser terrors of the lower slopes.

They could not go as fast this time; every step had to be made carefully. They had gotten halfway across when they heard a great cry behind them. They knew it was Kala, but they dared not look back. They could only proceed painfully along the knifelike edge of the ridge, keeping their eyes fixed on the lower end.

They had advanced only a few steps when they saw something that almost caused them to lose their precarious balance. Teekoos awaited them at the end of the ridge! He had reached the last ledge of the rock and his head stuck up over it, looking toward them. His face was contorted in a look of savage hate. Rimau knew that Teekoos had come to revenge himself on the chief through his children-and on Rimau too.

"Hold fast! Hold fast!" Rimau said to Paksa. "We shall make it. I shall take care of Teekoos." But he wondered how he could defend himself and still keep his balance. Only one hand was free.

Teekoos had pulled himself up to the ledge. He crouched, waiting, his belt knife in his hand—the same knife they had seen him smearing with poison by the river.

Suddenly they heard a loud snarl from below the ledge where Teekoos crouched. Teekoos heard the snarl too and turned toward it, but he was too late. Something orange and black flung itself upon the ledge, and there was a brief struggle on the edge of the shelf. Teekoos held to the rock with one hand, striking out at the tiger with his knife. The tiger pulled at him, raking him with his great claws.

"It is the young tiger!" Rimau said in astonishment. "The one that was caught in the trap!" The two boys watched breathlessly, as the fight grew more fierce. Teekoos could not hang on; his grip loosened, but he still fought the tiger. Spitting and roaring and screaming, Teekoos and the tiger rolled over and over on the tiny shelf of rock. Then they went over the side of the ledge, still locked in battle, and hurtled through the air down to the rocks below.

The two boys, with their precious burden, were still leaning far out from the sides of the ridge. They steadied themselves and slowly proceeded. When they reached the ledge, off which the man and the tiger had plunged, they rested a little, trying to overcome their dizziness and horror at what they had seen. They forgot for an instant what followed after them.

"That tiger must have been watching us too!" Rimau said, when he could control his voice.

The two boys looked about them and saw that out of the gray moss grew thousands of bell-like flowers of brilliant red. They had never seen such flowers before-the flowers of Nan-gir-Jati! Had they been there when they climbed the rock, they wondered. They must have been, but their anxiety had made them blind. Now they looked about in all directions. It was only then that they saw Kala. He was creeping along on the ridge toward them. He came slowly, but with a sureness that amazed them. He inched his way along, clinging to the knife-like edge of the rock with both hands. His face was purple with rage, and his mouth was distorted in frightful grimaces. Terrified, Rimau recalled his night encounter with this awful creature. His flesh crawled. The two boys started down the rock as fast as they could go. It was more difficult to descend than to climb, for it was hard not to look down into the fearful depths below. Rimau even forgot the weight of the sleeping child on his back.

Now Kala had reached the end of the ridge and was coming down faster than they. They could not escape him! They had paused too long on the rocky shelf. Now they would have to fight! They stopped, and Rimau said, "Give me your scarf. Let me tie Madoo to your back."

Thinking Rimau must be tired, Paksa handed him his scarf and allowed Rimau to fasten Madoo, still sleeping, to his back. As he tied the knot and twisted it with all his strength, Rimau whispered, "Now, hurry! Go down as fast as you can! I shall take care of Kala!"

"No!" said Paksa, when he saw what Rimau intended to do. "I shall stay and help you fight Kala!"

"You must go, Paksa," Rimau told him. "One of us must save Madoo."

There was no time to say more. Kala's cruel face leered just above them. Paksa swung himself swiftly from limb to limb and from root to root and disappeared in the leafy depths below.

For a few minutes Rimau kept barely out of the madman's reach. Then, coming to a wide shelf of rock, he stopped and wait-ed. Here the moss was thick and deep, affording a good foothold. Rimau knew that his strength was as nothing compared to that of the brute climbing down toward him. He also knew that Pak-sa was making his way down the mountain with Madoo safe on his back. He wanted to delay Kala as long as possible and give Paksa more time to reach the villagers below. All Paksa needed was time—a few more minutes. Then he would be safe.

The Tiger of Bitter Valley

The boy braced himself and waited. He had chosen a spot where his enemy must face him. He placed his back against the solid wall of rock. Within his reach was the limb of a large tree that grew out of the moss below the shelf of rock.

He saw the rough, bruised feet of the madman dangling over the rock above him. Kala quickly found a handhold and dropped down to the ledge. He glared at the boy and rushed at him.

Rimau ducked, and Kala failed to grasp him. Twice more he eluded his enemy. Then Kala's hands clutched the boy's shoulders, as they had on that night weeks ago on the path to the village. Now he knew the secret of those powerful hands. They had grown mighty from frequent crossings of the precipice above. Kala pulled Rimau toward him. The boy struggled, clinging to the limb of the tree. Then Kala gave a mighty jerk. Rimau let go, pushing against the madman with all his strength. Boy and man shot out over the shelf of rock and fell downward, whirling through creepers and branches of trees. Then Rimau knew nothing more.

13.
The Great Magic

WHEN RIMAU AWAKENED, HIS HEAD WAS throbbing, and he ached all over. He felt for his pillow, but his hand clutched soft moss. Where was he? His heart beat wildly, and he opened his eyes.

A few feet from him lay a still figure. With a wild bound of his heart, he remembered! He was on Nangir-Jati alone with Kala the madman. They had both hurtled down from the shelf of rock and now....

He felt his arms and legs. They seemed to be all right, but his head still ached and pounded. He must have struck it in the fall. He looked about him. They had not fallen all the way to the foot of Nangir-Jati but only to another ledge of the rock.

He wondered if Kala was dead. Painfully he got to his feet and moved very cautiously nearer the madman. Kala lay face upward on the moss. He was still, very still! The boy crept closer. He was afraid but curious. He saw the man's dirty, matted hair. He had been wounded in the head and blood flowed from a cut behind his right ear. His face was gray and lifeless. Rimau looked at Kala's hands—those dreadful iron claws that so often had grasped the sharp rock of the upper precipice. Now they lay limp and helpless.

116

Then Kala moaned, and the boy sprang to his feet. The man was still alive! Perhaps he would get up and leap on him! He stepped back, ready to continue down the rock as fast as he could go. Then he saw that one of Kala's legs was doubled back at a peculiar angle. It was surely broken! There was no danger of Kala's doing any damage now. He was bleeding a great deal. The boy remembered the tigress and realized she would soon find him.

Looking down at the injured man, Rimau thought of what Kala must have been like before he became mad. He remembered the words of Jimat: "Oh, he was one to take the heart!" And Toko-Batoo had said, "He was my dearest friend."

Rimau kneeled down again and turned Kala's head a little, so that he could examine the wound. It was bleeding profusely, and he pinched it together with his fingers. The flow of blood was staunched. Then he noticed, just above his fingers, an old scar-a scar from some previous wound. It was deep and long. It must have been a severe injury.

Rimau began to feel cramped and uncomfortable. He eased his knees under Kala's head, so that he held it in his lap. This position was more comfortable. He watched the slight rise and fall of the man's chest. His heart was beating; he still lived.

Then, from below him, he heard the sound of many voices, and felt a great flood of relief. The village men must have met Paksa and learned that Rimau was alone on the mountain with the madman. They were coming to his rescue. First one, and then another head appeared through the dense foliage. On every face he saw horror and dismay. Lips moved but spoke no word, for fear of the madman struck everyone dumb.

Finally the chief's head appeared. He looked in amazement at Rimau and the unconscious Kala. He came closer and saw what Rimau was doing. "Come away!" he commanded. "It is best like this—best for him and best for us." His voice was choked with grief, and he turned away.

Then the other men came to look. "Come with us," they urged. "Come while there is time!"

117

The Tiger of Bitter Valley

The boy seemed to hear them from a very long distance, and he saw them now but dimly. He looked only at the wound on Kala's head, which he still held between his fingers. His heart sank in despair. He had searched for Jimat's face among the villagers and had not found it. He did not look for Toko-Batoo. He knew Toko-Batoo was not yet strong enough to climb this rock. And Paksa would have gone on to the village with Madoo.

While the men stood in a circle, looking at Kala, he stirred and moaned again. A wave of fright stirred the company. "Come now—now!" they screamed. "We will not stay longer!"

"This man is badly hurt. He cannot possibly harm anyone." Rimau spoke at last. "We cannot leave him like this. The tigress is here on the rock. We must carry him to the village, where we can take care of him. Can't you see that his leg is broken?"

The men hesitated for a moment. Then, one by one, they slid back down the rock into the green jungle below. Rimau heard the echoes of their wild scramble down the mountain. Hopelessness engulfed him. He could not possibly carry Kala down the rock and through the jungle by himself. And although the man's leg was broken, he might be hard to manage when he regained consciousness. He felt great anger toward the villagers for their fear. He was afraid too, but he could not leave Kala to die on the rock. He decided that he would wait until Kala's wound stopped bleeding and he could let go of it. Then he would straighten his leg and find water for him. The spring they had found on the way up must be nearby.

Rimau began to plan what he might do to protect Kala and himself from the tigress. He knew she might be close to them. Perhaps she was watching them now; perhaps she could smell the fresh blood. He was sorry that it had not been the tigress that had gone over the precipice with Teekoos, instead of the young one. He could have fought the young tiger with his belt knife, and perhaps he could have killed it. He felt his knife with his free hand. It was a good Toba knife made of tempered steel with a sharp point and a thin blade. He laid it down in front of him on the moss.

He remembered the night he had slept in the cart by the shores of Lake Toba, when the tiger had come and licked his foot. He remembered how the savage beast had sniffed and sniffed and licked. Would the tigress do that when she came, he wondered.

Higher up on the rock toward his left, there was a slight sound. He let go of the wound on Kala's head and lay down beside him with his belt knife in his hand. It was his only chance. He froze in an attitude of unconsciousness, opening his eyes just once to look at Kala's wound. It did not seem to be bleeding much now.

The tigress came softly. Her great padded feet sank into the moss. Rimau felt her warm breath as she crept close, and her cool, damp fur brushed his face. He could hear her sniffing Kala, and then she began to lick the blood from his wound. At that instant the boy grasped his belt knife tighter. The tiger was directly over him. With all his strength he drove the knife into the tigress's chest. With a fierce roar and a convulsive shudder, the great cat sprang into the air and came down, clawing and spitting, right upon him. But she had received a death wound. Her struggles grew weaker, her clawing harmless, and at last she lay still. Rimau had been scratched in the face by her great claws and he was all but smothered by the great body on top of him. Then the throbbing in his head shut out all other sounds, and the blackness closed in on him again.

Was it a shout he heard in the distance, or was it another noise in his own head? He couldn't be sure. Then he opened his eyes and looked up into his uncle's anguished face.

With an exclamation of horror Jimat knelt down beside him and, with all his strength, pushed the body of the tigress until it rolled off the boy. Rimau felt the cool wetness of the big cat's blood all over his body. His uncle cried out again in great distress. Then Jimat saw the hilt of the belt knife protruding from the tigress's chest. He sank down on the ground with a sigh of relief.

119

"I am not much hurt," Rimau said. "Thanks be to every good spirit of this mountain!" Jimat exclaimed in an awed voice. Then he knelt over the boy and examined every scratch and claw mark. Satisfied that Rimau was not injured in any serious way, he turned his attention to Kala. He examined the wound on his head and straightened his leg. He leaned over the madman's chest and listened to his heartbeat.

"How can we get him back to the village?" the boy asked. The strength of his own voice surprised him. Since Jimat had come, he felt much better. He was sure now that they could carry Kala down the mountain. He sat up.

"Miserable cowards!" Jimat's face suddenly darkened with anger. "I met them coming down!" Then he looked at Rimau with wonder and affection. "You are well named, Menga-Rajah-Segala-Harimau!" he exclaimed. "You have proved that you are a Ruler of Tigers. But you could never have done it, had you not been trying to help Kala. I can see how it all happened."

Rimau got to his feet and looked down at the dead tigress. Then he saw the wound in her shoulder. "Look! Look!" he cried. "Teekoos did hit the tiger with his spear! She must have carried it away with her and brushed it off later." Then he remembered. "Did Paksa tell you about Teekoos?"

"Paksa told us," Jimat said, with wonder still showing in his face. "Paksa told us everything."

Jimat set about making bamboo splints for Kala's broken leg. "We shall pad it with soft moss now," the medicine man said. "When we get to the village we will use something else."

When the leg had been cared for, they began to make a litter of branches. They did not hurry, although the day was waning. They were no longer afraid of the tigress or her young one, and the madman of the mountain lay unconscious at their feet. Slowly and carefully they fashioned the litter so that two persons could manage it. They knew that it would take a long time to carry Kala home and that they would have to stop and rest often.

"I hope we can get him to the village before he wakes up," Jimat said. "We will have to take him to my house. No one else in the village will have him. Even his brother, Sutan Dolok, thinks he should be left here to die."

It was a slow, difficult task to carry the litter down the steep trail of Nangir-Jati. When they finally reached the foot of the great rock the sun had gone down, but they found the place where they had hidden on the tiger hunt and camped there.

Rimau went up the path to the spring. There he washed his sarong and drank the cool water. Then they built a fire and sat in the warm glow. They had wrapped their scarves about the wounded man, and Jimat brought water in a cup made of leaves and dripped some between Kala's lips. He swallowed it, and Jimat's eyes brightened with satisfaction. "He can swallow. He is thirsty. Perhaps he will get well."

As they sat there in the light of the fire, Rimau asked his uncle to look at the old deep scar on Kala's head.

"You know what I think?" Jimat exclaimed, after he had inspected it. "I think he must have gotten this after he left the village. I do not think he had it before he became mad."

"Could a heavy blow on the head have caused his madness?" Rimau wanted to know.

"I suppose it could have. How can we ever know?"

Toward morning the wounded man stirred and moaned. He spoke a few words, and Rimau leaned over him to hear what he said. "No, Teekoos! No, Teekoos!" Kala mumbled in a weak voice.

Rimau and Jimat looked at one another. They could hardly contain their amazement, but they did not speak, for Kala was mumbling more words. "Don't strike me!" The sick man cringed. "Don't strike me!" The two watchers listened and waited, but Kala said nothing more and soon sank again into unconsciousness.

As soon as there was light enough to see, Jimat and Rimau lifted the litter and made their way down the mountain. This was easy traveling compared to descending Nangir-Jati. They stopped often to rest, so it was late afternoon before they entered the village with their burden. They went directly to Jimat's house and laid Kala on a clean mat.

"Hurry with the rice pot, Rimau," said Jimat. "I must find clean rags for padding the splints and a soft pillow for Kala's head. And get a blanket from the chest." Jimat and Rimau did all they could for the injured man; then they took turns keeping watch over him.

The villagers had been terrified when they saw the boy and the witch doctor returning from the mountain with Kala. They had said that only great evil could come of it. But as time passed, they seemed to forget their fear and were stirred by great excitement. They often gathered outside Jimat's house.

On the third day after Kala was brought to Jimat's house he awakened and looked about him. When Rimau saw the sick man's eyes following him, he sensed at once that Kala was changed. There was no madness in his expression. There was only peace and gratitude. As they watched him, Kala spoke in a low, clear voice. "Where am I?" he asked. "Jimat, Jimat! Where am I?"

Jimat' s eyes filled with sudden tears, as he knelt beside Kala and took his hard, rough hand. "You are here in my house among good friends."

"Where have I been?" Kala asked. "Why did Teekoos strike me?"

"Teekoos is not here," Jimat said softly. "You are sick. You have been sick for a long time. Now you are getting well. You have nothing to be afraid of."

Kala smiled and dozed off in a natural sleep.

"I have heard stories of things like this," Jimat said. "Of how a blow on the head could cause madness. Then later on another injury near the same spot seemed to relieve the pressure and make the person sensible again."

They sat quietly for several minutes, marveling at what had happened. "I must call his brother and Toko-Batoo," Jimat said.

When Kala opened his eyes again he saw the familiar faces of his brother and his dearest friend. He looked from one to the other and spoke their names.

The chief fell to his knees and sobbed aloud. "We must call his wife and baby from her father's house," he said.

"I will send a messenger right now," Toko-Batoo said in a husky voice.

The next day a council was called. It was held in Jimat's house, because Jimat would not leave Kala. The villagers crowded into the room and sat with reverent faces.

The chief, dressed in his finest ceremonial robes, sat in a place of honor in the corner farthest away from the door of the room. He spoke in a strong voice: "People of Bitter Valley Village, many wonderful things have happened among us. We have come here now to honor the Great Ruler of all the Tigers." Then he beckoned to Rimau to come and sit beside him. Turning to the boy, Sutan Dolok spoke to him in the presence of all the people. "It is your magic that has done these great things. It was your magic that brought Madoo back. It was your magic that saved my brother Kala and brought him back to himself. It was your magic that destroyed the tigress and that showed me the strength and courage of my own son, Paksa." Then he added, "I am sure now that it was Teekoos who tried to destroy Kala and left him for dead on the mountain two years ago."

Then Jimat spoke in a strong voice. "It was Rimau's magic that saved your own life, too, but you didn't know it. Remember the day he flicked dust on the melon Teekoos divided with you? The knife that Teekoos had used to cut that melon was smeared with poison."

Sutan Dolok's face turned pale. He could not speak.

The village people crowded around Rimau with speeches of praise and thanksgiving for all he had done. The boy was embarrassed.

"Rimau's magic is the magic of the good spirits and the Great Good Spirit," Jimat said. "It is made of three things: courage, good sense, and kindness. Rimau has learned this magic well."

Rimau felt happy and proud when he heard these words. He wished that his father were with him now and might hear them too. He wished that he could tell his father about killing the tigress. It had now been four months since he had left his home. He longed to see his mother and his little sisters.

After the council was over, he spoke to his uncle. "Do you think my magic is strong enough for me to return to my village? Do you think it is strong enough to protect me from Gadoh?"

"I will go with you to your village," Jimat said. "I have not seen my sister for many years. I will ask the chief when we may start."

As soon as Kala could sit up and feed himself, he was moved to his own house, where his wife and his brother's family cared for him with great joy. His leg was healing. Jimat was sure that by the time he returned from his trip, the splints could be taken off. Soon Kala would walk and be a strong man again. Even now he could sit up and move about a little.

On a sunny morning Jimat and Rimau left Bitter Valley Village. Almost everyone in the village accompanied the travelers as far as the tiger pit. There Rimau sadly said good-by to Paksa and his family and to Toko-Batoo. Then the villagers turned back.

It was early evening ten days later when the two travelers entered Rocky Hills Village. They hurried at once to the house of Chief Feermin. At the foot of the ladder that led up into the great house, they stopped and called. A voice answered—the chief's voice.

They climbed the ladder and stood in the council room. Chief Feermin looked at them with unbelieving eyes.

"I have brought the young chief back," Jimat said.

At the sound of his voice Rimau's mother came running into the room. With tears in her eyes she welcomed her son and her brother. The house was filled with rejoicing. The two little girls scurried into Rimau's arms, and he held them fast, as though he would never let them go.

As they sat around the oil lamp, Jimat told of all the adventures that had befallen Rimau in Bitter Valley. It was a long story, and the chief stopped him often to ask questions.

"Now," the medicine man concluded, "the young chief has shown himself to be the master of tigers and men. I think there is nothing in this village that can withstand his magic."

"There is nothing!" the chief replied. "I was going to dispatch a messenger this very day to bring him home." His eyes rested on his only son with joy and pride. "Gadoh is just recovering from a severe attack of *chachar* sickness. It has left him almost blind, and his face is terribly scarred. He is changed; he is now a very humble man."

So Rimau came home to his own country with his great magic. And he has shown ever since to the villagers of Rocky Hills the good sense, the kindness, and the courage that made him the Tiger of Bitter Valley.

About the Author

During her adventurous life, Norma Youngberg was a prolific writer and creative writing teacher. Her classic books such as Queen's Gold, Jungle Thorn, Tiger of Bitter Valley, Singer on the Sand, Headhunter Hostage, and many others reveal the power of the gospel among primitive jungle peoples, and are favorites still today. Norma was born in Iowa and grew up in South Dakota. She came from a family of teachers, missionaries, and writers. Norma and husband Gustavus spent 20 years in the mission field, raised a family of six, and pioneered work among headhunters on the Tatau River of Sarawak.

We invite you to view the complete
selection of titles we publish at:

www.TEACHServices.com

Scan with your mobile
device to go directly
to our website.

Please write or email us your praises, reactions, or
thoughts about this or any other book we publish at:

TEACH Services, Inc.
P U B L I S H I N G
www.TEACHServices.com

P.O. Box 954
Ringgold, GA 30736

info@TEACHServices.com

TEACH Services, Inc., titles may be purchased in bulk for
educational, business, fund-raising, or sales promotional use.
For information, please e-mail:

BulkSales@TEACHServices.com

Finally, if you are interested in seeing
your own book in print, please contact us at

publishing@TEACHServices.com

We would be happy to review your manuscript for free.